TIMAEUS

The Library of Liberal Arts
OSKAR PIEST, FOUNDER

TIMAEUS

PLATO

Translated by
BENJAMIN JOWETT
With an Introduction by
GLENN R. MORROW

Macmillan Publishing Company
New York
Collier Macmillan Publishers
London

CONTENTS

SELECTED BIBLIOGRAPHY

Bury, R. G., *Timaeus*. Greek text, English translation, introduction and notes (In Volume VII of Plato in the Loeb Classical Library). Cambridge, Mass., 1929.

Cornford, F. M., *Plato's Cosmology*. The *Timaeus* translated with a running commentary. New York, 1937.

Martin, T. Henri, *Etudes sur le Timée de Platon*. Two volumes. Paris, 1841.

Rivaud, Albert, *Timée*. Greek text, French translation, and introduction. (In Volume X of the Budé edition of Plato). Paris, 1925.

Robin, Léon, *Etudes sur la signification et la place de la physique dans la philosophie de Platon*. Paris, 1919.

Shorey, Paul, "The Interpretation of the *Timaeus*," and "The *Timaeus* of Plato," in *American Journal of Philology*, IX (1888), 395-418; and X (1889), 45-78.

Taylor, A. E., *A Commentary on Plato's Timaeus*. Oxford, 1928.

Taylor, A. E., *Plato: the Man and his Work*. New York, 1927. Pp. 436-460.

Zeller, E., *Plato and the Older Academy*. New York, 1888. Pp. 293-434.

INTRODUCTION

I

The *Timaeus* belongs to the very latest group of Plato's writings, and was almost certainly composed after 360 B.C., when he was nearing seventy years of age. Though cast in the familiar dialogue form, this composition ceases to be a dialogue after the first few pages, and becomes a continuous discourse by Timaeus on the origin and nature of the world. This Timaeus is a citizen of Locri, a city in southern Italy, and he is apparently on a visit to Athens. He is described as being rich and wellborn, as having held important offices at Locri, and as being well versed in the knowledge of nature and eminent in philosophy. Whether there ever lived a real person answering to this name and description is very doubtful.[1] It is probable that Plato invented Timaeus to serve as a mouthpiece for his own ideas, like the Athenian Stranger in the *Laws*, and the Eleatic Stranger in the *Sophist* and *Statesman*. The other personages introduced in the opening pages are three in number. Hermocrates has usually been identified, though for no very compelling reason, with the Syracusan statesman and general of that name who played an important part in the defeat of the Athenian expedition against Syracuse (415-413 B.C.). Critias is an Athenian, and an old man. Hence he cannot be identified with the Critias who led the Thirty Tyrants at Athens after the surrender to Sparta in 404 B.C. The Critias of our dialogue is perhaps the grandfather of that Critias, Plato's own great-grandfather. The other participant in the opening conversation is Socrates. As in all the other dialogues of this period, except the *Philebus*, Socrates is no longer the mouthpiece of Plato's ideas; though it is

[1] There is extant a treatise *On the Soul of the World and Nature* by a Timaeus of Locri; but it is now generally recognized to be a composition of the first century, and to be mainly a paraphrase of Plato's *Timaeus*, done in pseudo-Doric dialect.

significant that the theme of Timaeus' discourse, and of the other discourses to follow, grows out of a challenge presented by him to his three companions. The conversation takes place at Athens; and if we must set an imaginary date for it, we can most appropriately choose a time shortly before 421 B.C., when Athens was at peace and visitors from the west, such as Timaeus and Hermocrates, would be welcome.

The *Timaeus* was originally intended, as we can see from the opening pages, to be the first of a trilogy of dialogues. It was to be followed by the *Critias*, which was left uncompleted at Plato's death, and by a *Hermocrates*, which seems never to have been begun. The plan of the trilogy can be roughly inferred from the opening conversation. On the previous day Socrates has given his three companions an account of the ideal state, and has expressed his desire to see this state brought out of the realm of abstraction and portrayed in action. Feeling himself incapable of this task, he has appealed to his three friends, whose scientific attainments, coupled with their experience in public affairs, have given them the ability to take part at once "both in politics and in philosophy." After consultation they have devised the following program. Timaeus, who is the most versed in astronomy and cosmology, is to speak first of the generation of the world and the nature of man. Critias is to follow with an ancient legend which he heard in his youth concerning the mighty exploits of the Athenians who lived "before the great deluge." According to this legend, these ancient Athenians had institutions comparable to those described in Socrates' picture of the ideal state, and they gave splendid evidence of their virtue in turning back an invasion from the island of Atlantis, whose inhabitants were threatening to conquer all Europe and Asia. We are not told what was to be the theme of Hermocrates' discourse. But it is clear that the central theme of the trilogy is a political one. It attacks the problem with which Plato was so deeply concerned in his later years—how to translate his political ideals into living historical reality. It may at first blush seem strange that such a theme should be introduced by a discourse on cosmology. But the relation of the *Timaeus* to the larger plan, and its aptness as an introduction, will become evident as we come to understand it.

This dialogue is the only writing of Plato's devoted to what we would now call natural science. Its purpose is to describe the generation of the universe—the "heaven" or the "cosmos"—through an analysis of the factors that make it what it is. This theme was not a novel one in the fourth century. In one fashion or another almost all of Plato's predecessors, from Thales in the sixth century to Democritus in the fourth, had tried to explain how the world came to be and what the fundamental principles or elements are on which it depends. But Plato's handling of this theme is strikingly different, in two important respects, from the treatment of it by his predecessors. In the first place, his predecessors (with few exceptions) had thought of these inquiries into nature as giving us genuine knowledge. Plato asserts that there can be no knowledge, in the strict sense of the word, of the sense-world. The only objects of knowledge are the Ideas; they alone possess the permanence, intelligibility, and demonstrable interconnections which will yield the certainty of scientific understanding. The Ideas alone are true Being; and science is of Being. The sense-world, on the other hand, is the sphere of Becoming, that is, of ceaseless change; and any account of Becoming can be no more than a "probable tale," or myth ($\mu\tilde{\upsilon}\theta o s$). "As Being is to Becoming, so is knowledge to belief." This is why Timaeus, at the outset of his discourse, warns his hearers against expecting more exactness and consistency than the subject he is dealing with permits. "Enough, if we adduce probabilities as likely as any others" (29b).

But we must not be misled into thinking that the "myth" which Timaeus recounts is for Plato merely an idle fiction. Timaeus elsewhere asserts that his account of the cosmos is "as probable as any other—or rather, more probable" (48d). Plato seems to be inviting comparison with his predecessors, and asking whether his account is not more credible than theirs. If, contrary to Plato's practice, we call such inquiries scientific, then Plato's account is intended to be a contribution to natural science, of the same order as the work of Anaxagoras, or Empedocles, or Democritus. The scope of his inquiries is the same as theirs—extending from the phenomena of the heavens, the motions of the planets, the nature of the primary bodies and their various transformations, down to the physiology of man, the mechanism of perception, and the nature of disease. He draws freely from his predecessors, though not from all of them equally, exhibiting a decided preference for the theories of Empedocles and the Pythagoreans. Above all, he shows his familiarity with the most recent scientific developments of his day, such as the mathematical theory of proportion, the doctrine of the five regular solids, and the theory of celestial circles advanced to account for the seemingly erratic movement of the planets. His successors in antiquity had no hesitation in turning to the *Timaeus* for a statement of what Plato believed on matters of natural science, though they were inclined to overlook Plato's warning that he is expounding beliefs, not science.

The second respect in which Plato's account differs from the cosmology of his predecessors is its teleology. The course of physical inquiry prior to Plato had culminated in the atomic theory of Democritus—a conception of the cosmos as the necessary and undesigned result of the collisions of eternally moving particles. It has sometimes been asserted that Plato was not acquainted with this theory, because he never refers to Democritus by name. But it would be very strange if he was ignorant of a doctrine so well known to Aristotle, and besides, his own account of the ultimate constituents of the primary bodies (53c-57c) reads like a deliberately presented alternative to the atomic theory of matter. In any case he was well acquainted with the mechanistic trend of earlier cosmology, and critical of it. In the *Phaedo*, Socrates is portrayed as giving an account of his early interest in these "inquiries about nature," and of his eventual dissatisfaction because they took no account of the "good." Even Anaxagoras, who asserted that Nous (Mind) is the ordering cause of all things, disappointed him. "I found the man making no use of mind, nor of any other principle of order in things, but appealing only to 'airs' and 'ethers' and 'waters' and the like." It is as if someone had said that intelligence is the cause of Socrates' actions, but had then tried to explain his being in prison as the consequence of the structure of his bones and muscles, neglecting the true cause, which is that Socrates had thought it better to remain and undergo the penalty than to escape to Megara or Boeotia. To call his bones and muscles the causes of Socrates' actions is absurd. They are indeed conditions without which he could not do what seemed best; but the true cause is "the choice of the best." Likewise in cosmology the real cause is not the "vortex," as Anaxagoras seemed to think, but the power which arranges things for the best. "It is the good that embraces and binds things together" (*Phaedo*, 96a-99d).

True to the principles laid down in the *Phaedo*, the *Timaeus* asserts that the visible world is a creation, made in the likeness of an eternal pattern, by a cause working for the best. The nature of this cause, the "maker and father of the universe," is hard to discover; but his activity is described as that of an artificer, or craftsman (δημιουργός, demiurge), who brings orderly structure out of disorderly materials, and fashions them into as perfect a likeness of his pattern as their nature permits. The figure of the craftsman is no doubt a metaphor and should not be pressed too closely. But it must be taken as expressing Plato's belief that the intelligence which is the cause of our world is at least as clear-sighted about its purposes, and exercises as much foresight and design in the choice of means, as we find in the procedure of a competent craftsman. Nothing less than this will do justice to the order and beauty of the world, which is "the fairest of creations."

This was a bold and novel conception. To conceive of the world as coming into being like the planned production of a work of art implies teleology of the most conscious and clear-sighted sort. Plato was not impressed by a merely biological teleology of "unconscious purposiveness," of which there are traces in earlier thought, and which apparently satisfied Aristotle. In putting forth this radically teleological view of the universe, Plato had to set aside both the cosmology of previous philosophers, and the cosmogonies of popular mythology. And yet his doctrine was deeply rooted in a feeling common to both the myth-makers and the philosophers of Greece, the feeling of a fundamental kinship between man and nature, or, as the philosophers put it, between the "little cosmos" which is man and the larger cosmos that includes him. For Plato it was not only intellectually more satisfying, but it was also aesthetically and morally necessary, that the cause of the universe should manifest the same desire for order and beauty that man finds within his own soul.

But in asserting teleology Plato does not forget mechanism. In fact, the greatness of the *Timaeus* consists precisely in its recognition of the immense, though subordinate, role played by the "auxiliary causes," as they are called here. In the generation of the world the creator does not begin from nothing, nor operate on materials created by himself. The creator of the world, like the artisan of common experience, must exercise his skill upon the materials available. These materials are not always the best adapted to his purposes, and in some cases they offer resistance to his efforts. Consequently, if we wish to understand his work, we have to know not only the eternal pattern which he is following, but also the auxiliary causes by which he accomplishes his ends. This distinction between the true or divine cause and the secondary or auxiliary causes is brought out emphatically in the very structure of the dialogue. In the first part of his discourse, Timaeus describes the operation of the creator in giving the world the most perfect shape, the spherical, in endowing it with a soul guided by intelligence and duly created in accordance with mathematical proportion, and in populating it with the various kinds of living beings, including man, whose soul partakes of the same harmonious proportions as the world-soul, and whose body is equipped with sense-organs for apprehending the cosmic order. So far the emphasis has been on the goodness of the maker's intentions and the perfection of the pattern he is following; the materials he has to employ have been taken for granted, and without analysis. At this point (48a) Timaeus breaks the course of his exposition and makes what he calls a "new beginning," in order to take account of "the nature of fire, and water, and air, and earth, such as they were prior to the creation of the heavens." These materials, and the receptacle—or space—in which they operate, are possessed of inherent powers, moving and being moved by one another "without reason or measure." This is what Plato calls the realm of necessity; here what happens is due, not to design, but to blindly operating motions and powers.

The role of these powers is enormous, and almost all the remainder of the dialogue is concerned with them. They explain the mechanism of vision; the motions of the primary bodies and their transformations into one another; the varieties of fluids and metals;

the phenomena of melting and cooling, of freezing and thawing; the varieties and compounds of earth; the tactile qualities of hot and cold, heavy and light; tastes, odors, sounds, colors and the feelings of pleasure and pain; the human body, with its structure of bone, marrow, flesh and sinews; the mechanism of respiration; the movement of the blood and the other body fluids; and the various diseases that afflict the human frame. Much of this detail is of interest today only to the historian of science. Natural science has advanced so far since Plato's day that it is even difficult for a modern student to imagine how some of these "explanations" could have once been seriously entertained. But it should be remembered that Plato himself realized how tentative his theories were. He was perhaps more clearly aware of the provisional and uncertain character of natural science than are many of its practitioners today. And there is an unmistakable hardness in Plato's procedure. In dealing with these "works of necessity" he tries to picture as clearly as possible the particular way in which the operating powers produce, or could be conceived as producing, the observed effects—as, for instance, in his explanation of respiration, in his account of concordant sounds, and in his theory of diseases. There is an obvious similarity with the spirit of modern science in Plato's attempt to provide a mathematical explanation, wherever possible. The most striking example of this is his discussion of the four primary bodies. Unfortunately the sense-world only rarely permits of explanation in the clear terms of mathematics; and this is one reason why, for Plato, it is the realm of opinion and belief, not science.

How does the Demiurge make use of these auxiliary causes? Plato tells us that Nous, the ruling power, "persuaded" necessity to bring the greatest part of created things to perfection (48a). This is another metaphor, but an apt one. Persuasion, of course, is different from compulsion. Every craftsman knows that he cannot force his materials to take on forms or perform functions that go against their nature. What he employs is intelligence. He selects among the materials available those best adapted to his purpose, and these he handles with discrimination, utilizing certain of their powers, while ignoring or subordinating the others. Persuasion, however, is a term that suggests rhetoric, rather than intelligence or integrity; and we know that Plato in the *Gorgias* was severely critical of the so-called art of persuasion cultivated by the sophists and politicians of his day. But in a later dialogue, the *Phaedrus*, he himself sets forth the principles of a genuine art of persuasion. The orator must know the good, he says, so as not to mislead his audience; and he must know also the souls of his hearers, so as to know what desires and interests are present in them and may be appealed to effectively. Persuasion, then, in its broadest sense, is the technique of intelligence; it is the proper means for accomplishing what we will with others—whether men or inanimate materials—by understanding them so thoroughly that we can use the forces inherent in them to bring about the end we desire. Naturally the divine craftsman, being "the best of causes," will not misuse his art of persuasion.

Furthermore, if we remember the political problem to which the *Timaeus* is a prelude, we will see additional significance in Plato's mention of persuasion as the method used by the Demiurge. The problem of the statesman is essentially one of producing order among his human materials, and is therefore a part of, and analogous to, the problem of the divine craftsman in ordering the cosmos. The statesman will succeed, presumably, only if he uses the same method of persuasion to bring about unity and harmony in his state. This theme is central in the *Laws*, and, as Cornford points out,[2] it is an echo of the famous reconciliation scene in the *Eumenides* of Aeschylus, where the forces of lawless vengeance are "persuaded" by Athena to subordinate themselves to the orderly processes of justice.

But persuasion has its limits. Plato's God is not omnipotent, as is the God of Hebrew and Christian theology. The divine craftsman frequently finds himself hampered by the imperfection of his materials, and by a certain incorrigibility resident in them. His aim always is to realize the good, but we are reminded again and again that his achievement is limited by what is possible. There remains inevitably a residue of imperfection in the created world. "It is impossible," says Plato in the *Theaetetus* (176a), "that evils should cease to be . . . Of necessity they haunt mortal nature and this region of ours." The *Timaeus* shows us what this

[2] *Plato's Cosmology*, pp. 361ff.

necessity is. Evil is due, not to the will or design of the Creator, but to the character of the materials upon which he works. God is the author only of good, as Plato had affirmed long before in the canons of theology laid down in the *Republic*.

II

To sum up, the factors that Plato regards as necessary for explaining the origin and nature of the cosmos are three: (1) the eternal pattern; (2) the materials, including the receptacle, or space, in which these materials and their powers are displayed; and (3) the Demiurge, who by his intelligence brings about in the receptacle the nearest likeness of the pattern which it is possible to produce. We recognize at once that the eternal pattern is what Plato has usually called Ideas, and described as the genuine reality which sensible objects in space and time imitate. There is relatively little discussion of the Ideas in the *Timaeus*. After all, Plato has discussed that doctrine often in other dialogues, and this is a discourse on cosmology. But we should not forget that the Ideas are important here also. At the very beginning of his discourse (27e), Timaeus distinguishes between "that which always is and has no becoming," and "that which is always becoming and never is"—a clear reference to the familiar distinction between the intelligible and the sense-worlds. Later (51c) he explicitly raises the question (evidently a controversial one) whether there are any "intelligible essences" apart from the sensible objects we perceive, and briefly but confidently justifies his assertion of their existence. Thus the doctrine of Ideas, though deliberately subordinated to other matters, is presupposed throughout this dialogue and in fact is fundamental to any real understanding of it.

But how are we to interpret the Demiurge? Plato mentions the cosmic craftsman not only here but also in the myth of the *Statesman* (273b, d; cf. 269d) and in the *Sophist* (265c). Is this merely a poetic metaphor, or does it represent some real cosmic agency distinct from the Ideas? Aristotle often criticizes Plato's Ideas for not providing any explanation of generation. The Ideas are not, and cannot be, efficient causes, he says; but an efficient cause is necessary, if we are to explain how the sense-world imitates the Ideas. Undoubtedly Plato himself was aware of this difficulty and it seems that his later doctrine of the soul as the "source of motion" was intended to meet it. The *Phaedrus*—and later the *Laws*—argues that all motion eventually presupposes something that is capable of moving itself, and that this self-moving agency is soul. Here then is the efficient cause that Aristotle demanded. For Plato the soul possesses not only the capacity of moving itself, and thus of initiating physical change; it is also the principle of knowing, that is, it can apprehend the intelligible world. The soul thus forms a kind of intermediary between the Ideas and the sense-world, being identical with neither. Such an intermediary role seems to be the function of the Demiurge in the *Timaeus*.

But to identify the Demiurge with soul *tout court* is impossible. For the Demiurge is described as himself creating soul, first the world-soul and then the soul of man. A tempting solution of this difficulty is to distinguish between Nous and the other ingredients of soul, and to identify the Demiurge with Nous, in particular with the Nous in the world-soul. The Demiurge will then not be identical with soul in all her aspects, united as she is with the world's body and spread out in space, but only with the reasoning faculty in the world-soul. This does not entirely remove the difficulty, since it implies that a part of the world-soul creates the whole. But we cannot hope altogether to lift the veil of allegory in which Plato has clothed his thought, and perhaps the implication just mentioned should not be taken too literally. The solution suggested accords with the *Philebus* (26e-28e), which identifies the "cause" and "demiurge" with Nous, which Socrates says is acknowledged by all wise men to be "king of heaven and earth." In any case, we can hardly escape the conclusion that the Demiurge, though a mythical figure, represents a real factor in the cosmos: he is the creative activity of Nous, distinct from the world because he is its creator; and distinguished from the Ideas, as the knowing subject is distinguished from the object known.[3]

[3] From this it is but a step to the view, adopted by Plutarch and many Christian Platonists, that the Ideas are thoughts in the mind of God. This,

This, it would seem, is Plato's God, viewed sometimes impersonally as pure reason, and at other times mythically as "maker and father."

But why should Nous concern itself with this region of Becoming? Why should there be a cosmos at all? Because, Plato says simply, the Creator was good, and desired that all things should be as like himself as they could be (29e). This was a new and momentous contribution to theology. Greek mythology frequently pictured the gods as jealous of human prosperity, and inclined to punish men who tried to rise above their human lot. Plato's doctrine here is an explicit denial of this article of Greek theology. "There is no place for jealousy in the chorus of the gods" (*Phaedrus*, 247a). But the positive side of Plato's doctrine is even more momentous. Xenophanes and Empedocles had, like Plato, criticized traditional theology for ascribing human imperfections to the gods, and had attained to the conception of God as one, as a "sacred and unutterable mind ($\phi\rho\acute{\eta}\nu$)." But no one prior to Plato had advanced the conception of a God whose perfection is outgoing, whose very nature leads him to work for the perfecting of other beings beneath him. This seems to have too lofty a conception even for Aristotle. Like Plato's God, the God of Aristotle is best described as Nous, the realization of all intelligible perfection; but he remains absorbed in the contemplation of his own intellectual nature. The world loves him, but he cares not for the world. Plato's thought lived after him, however, in the Stoic doctrine of Providence, and in the Neo-Platonic explanation of the world as an "emanation" from the One. And Christian theologians have usually interpreted Plato's utterance as a partial anticipation of their own doctrine of God's sacrificial love for the world.

The elaborate description of the creation of soul (34c-36e) is difficult to comprehend, and has been the theme of almost endless comment and controversy. The reader who approaches it for the first time will be helped in understanding it if he bears in mind that the soul is to be so constituted as to have a kind of existence intermediate between Being and Becoming. Its three basic ingre-

however, threatens the objectivity and independence of the Ideas upon which Plato always insists.

dients are being (or "essence," as Jowett translates the term οὐσία), sameness, and otherness—the three basic categories discussed in the *Sophist*. The being which enters into the making of the world-soul is a mixture of the indivisible and divisible kinds of being. "Indivisible being" is the kind of existence that belongs to the eternal Ideas, each of which is one, as contrasted with "divisible being," the many separate images of this Idea existing in space and time. Sameness and otherness can also be explained by reference to the *Sophist*, where we learn that "the other" is a necessary constituent of any differentiated world, that is, any world in which some things "are not" others. Partaking of these ingredients, therefore, the soul is enabled to make true affirmations (by virtue of "the same"), and true negative judgments (by virtue of the otherness in its composition) concerning both the divisible and the indivisible forms of being. It is at home, so to speak, in both the ideal and the sensible worlds. For the further clarification of these symbolical ingredients, as well as for the understanding of the mathematical proportions in the world-soul and their significance, the student should consult one of the commentaries in the Bibliography.[4] There he will also learn that the description of the circular motions in the world-soul is Plato's solution of one of the lively astronomical problems of his day, that of describing in mathematical terms the motions of the heavenly bodies, and in particular of accounting for the apparent irregularities in the motions of the "wanderers," that is, the planets.

Almost equally intriguing is Plato's account (49a-52c) of the receptacle (ὑποδοχή), or nurse (τιθήνη), of all generation. Plato insists that to understand the material factors in the sense-world something more fundamental is required than fire, air, water and earth, which were often regarded as the primary or elemental kinds of body. These are not the ultimate principles of the material world, for they are always undergoing change, sometimes seeming even to change into one another; and hence no one of them can be said to be itself rather than something else, or even to *be* at all. Nor is it enough to affirm the reality of Ideas of fire,

[4] E.g., Taylor, pp. 109-174; Cornford, pp. 57-94; Rivaud, pp. 39-63.

air, and the rest, of which the sensible fire and air are imitations. For an image must not only be *of* something; it must also be *in* something, and occur some*where*. Hence the necessity of a third factor, an enduring substratum in which the sensible fire, air and the rest occur. This substratum must itself be without form or quality, in order that it may be receptive to all the forms and qualities that are to be imaged in it. Because of its formlessness and indeterminateness, the receptacle cannot be apprehended by sense, nor even by reason; it can only be affirmed as something that must be assumed if Becoming is to occur (52c). It is likened to a nurse, or mother (50d), because its role in generation is passive, as compared with the Ideas, the paternal factor that gives form to the offspring. The receptacle is eternal, as eternal as the pattern; but it is distinct from the pattern, just as it is distinct from the images of the pattern to which it affords a place of occurrence. This doctrine of the receptacle—or as Plato eventually calls it, space ($\chi\acute{\omega}\rho\alpha$)—is important in that it cuts underneath all earlier attempts to find a substantial reality in the material bodies of sense-experience, or in any similarly material elements of which they are composed. It points forward to Aristotle's conception of "prime matter," and even farther, to the "idealization" of matter that characterizes the physics of modern times.

As for the so-called primary bodies—fire, air, earth and water—Plato advances the theory (which he admits is unfamiliar, $\dot{\alpha}\acute{\eta}\theta\eta s$) that their specific and distinguishing qualities are due to differences in mathematical (that is, geometrical) structure (53c-57d). Each of the four primary bodies is identified with one of the regular solids, and an elaborate mathematical theory is constructed to explain their various sub-forms and their transformations into one another. This looks like an attempt to present an alternative to the theory of Democritus, whose elemental particles were thought of as varying indefinitely in shape, and as combining with or separating from one another without rhyme or reason. In any case, it shows that Plato thinks of the formative action of Nous as extending down into the very raw material of Becoming, and fashioning it in accordance with intelligible patterns. Here again Plato's hypothesis anticipates a fundamental principle of modern physics, which has been inclined, ever since Galileo, to find the ultimate secret of physical nature in mathematically ordered structure.

Thus far we have left untouched a question which is likely to occur very early to any reader of the *Timaeus*, and which we know was much debated in ancient times. In speaking of the creation or generation of the cosmos, does Plato mean to imply that the cosmos had a beginning in time, or is it eternal? The discourse of Timaeus sets forth the generation of the world in the form of a story of successive actions performed by the Demiurge. But one of these actions of the Demiurge is the creation of time, with the establishment of the periodic revolutions of the heavenly bodies. The view most commonly accepted in antiquity was that the creation in time is an expository artifice. Aristotle expresses the traditional view neatly: "They [that is, Xenocrates and the Platonists] say that in describing the generation of the world they are doing just as a geometer does when he draws his figures, not implying that the world came into being at a certain time, but for purposes of exposition and clearer understanding exhibiting the world, as the geometer does his figure, in process of construction" (*On the Heavens* 279b33). If this is the correct interpretation, as it almost certainly is, then the story of the creation in time is one of the mythical features of the dialogue. Plato's real purpose is to set forth in intelligible order the factors that make the visible world what it is. The cosmos has always existed, and its cause is not a creator, in the Biblical sense, but a sustaining and continuously acting source of order and beauty.

III

The account of creation culminates in the creation of man (41b-47c, 69a-90d), the being whose history and prospects are to be the theme of the two following discourses in the trilogy. The picture of man presented in the *Timaeus* is in its main outlines the same as that in Plato's earlier dialogues, though Plato's emphasis here is upon the bodily vehicle, rather than the soul which uses it. As in the *Republic*, man's soul is composite, consisting of a divine part, the reason, and two "mortal parts," spirit and appetite.

The *Republic* had taught the sovereignty of the rational part over the rest. In similar vein the *Timaeus* describes how the immortal part, the reason, was made by the Demiurge himself, and from the same ingredients as were used in the making of the world-soul, though much diluted. To the "created gods," acting as his agents, the Demiurge entrusted the making of the mortal parts of man's soul and the body in which they are housed. Thus reason is the truly divine element in man, though all his other parts and powers are indirectly related to the divine Nous, and show evidence of its beneficent foresight. This part of the *Timaeus* is particularly instructive as to the way in which Plato employs both purpose and mechanism as explanatory factors. For instance, man was provided with an upright posture and organs of vision in order that he might "behold the courses of intelligence in the heavens," and thus rise to philosophy, "than which no greater good ever was or will be given by the gods to mortal man" (47b). At the same time the "fire" by which vision is effected is discussed at length, with the warning that such materials and processes are auxiliary to the true cause, intelligent purpose. So Timaeus proceeds through the rest of man's anatomy and physiology, pointing out, along with his analysis of the works of necessity, many arrangements designed to facilitate the victory of the rational soul and avert from man "all but self-inflicted evils."

Through all the physiological and anatomical details in this portion of the *Timaeus* there runs that note of pity for man to which Plato so often gives expression in his latest dialogues. "Man is a puppet of the gods," he writes in the *Laws* (644e). So here Timaeus describes, in terms moving in their very restraint, the creation of man's mortal nature:

Now of the divine, he himself was the creator, but the creation of the mortal he committed to his offspring. And they, imitating him, received from him the immortal principle of the soul; and around this they proceeded to fashion a mortal body, and made it to be the vehicle of the soul, and constructed within the body a soul of another nature which was mortal, subject to terrible and irresistible affections—first of all, pleasure, the greatest incitement to evil; then, pain, which deters from good; also rashness and fear, two foolish counselors, anger hard to be appeased, and hope easily led astray— these they mingled with irrational sense and with all-daring love according to necessary laws, and so framed man (69cd).

But along with this note of Olympian compassion there is a sterner theme. As always, Plato is determined to identify the forces that prevent man's realizing the happiness and perfection of which he is capable, and to find a remedy for them in nurture and education. "No man is voluntarily bad," he asserts once again (86e). Men's folly, ill-temper, despondency, rashness, cowardice, lust, and all the other distempers of their souls are in the main traceable to defective bodily constitution and bad education. And this, strangely enough, is why their position is not hopeless. The lesson of our whole discourse has been that reason is the sovereign and ordering principle, and this principle is in man as well as in the cosmos. In a bold metaphor Plato describes man as "a plant whose roots are in heaven," deriving from above the nourishment that feeds the divine and sovereign part of him (90a). It is therefore man's privilege, as well as his obligation, to imitate the reason in the cosmos, and bring order into his little province of the visible world. Thus he will be cooperating with the "maker and father" in fashioning the world into a mere perfect likeness of the eternal pattern.

IV

In Plato's *Timaeus* we have the first appearance of the legend of the lost island Atlantis which has so intrigued the imaginations of historians and explorers. Is it a pure fiction, or did Plato base his story upon fragments of oral tradition that have a foundation in fact? The opinion of the ancients seems to have been divided. Aristotle regarded it as a fiction, but others took it to be serious history. The latter seems to have been the prevailing view, even in modern times, until relatively recently. To complicate the question, geological evidence has been advanced for the existence in the quaternary period of an island or chain of islands west of the Straits of Gibraltar.[5] However that may be, the catastrophe that submerged these islands occurred long before the appearance of man on the earth, and hence long before recorded history. Not even the ancient records of the Egyptians, to which Plato professes to appeal, would carry us so far back. It is clear that Plato could

[5] For this see Rivaud, pp. 29-30.

not have been relying upon any written or oral tradition. The hypothesis now generally accepted is that the story was invented by Plato, out of fragments of geographical lore, legends of exotic nations and peoples, observations of the instability of the earth, and above all, from memories and traditions of the Persian Wars. The parallel between the exploits of the antediluvian Athenians in turning back the invasion from Atlantis, and the glorious exploits of the men of Marathon and Plataea in saving Greece from the Persians, is too close to have been an accident. The brief account of these heroic deeds, with the awe-inspiring catastrophe that followed them, serves the dramatic purpose of tying this dialogue to the *Critias*, which is to tell the story more fully. What is more important, it prepares our imaginations, through this excursion into the ancient human past, for the still more daring flight back to the beginning of time when the world itself was coming into being. With superb literary art Plato has converted an incredible story into history so credible that each successive generation of readers has difficulty persuading itself that it is not true.

V

Since the time of Aristotle the *Timaeus* has been regarded, and rightly so, as one of the most important of Plato's works. Aristotle refers to it more often than to any other Platonic dialogue. Crantor, a pupil of Xenocrates, wrote a commentary on it, the first of a long succession of Greek commentaries that ends only with Proclus, in the fifth century A.D. It was almost the only work of Plato known to Europe in the Middle Ages, and formed an indispensable part of the library of the scholastics, who valued it not merely as an epitome of Plato's philosophy, but also as a compendium of natural science. Its importance in the Renaissance is emphatically shown in Raphael's School of Athens, where Plato is pictured holding in his hand a volume labeled *Timeo*. With the revival of natural science, and the discovery by the western world of the complete body of Plato's writings, the *Timaeus* has been relatively less studied, though it has never ceased to attract the earnest attention of students of Plato and of philosophy generally. The late Professor Whitehead, so one of his students has told me, referred to the *Timaeus* frequently in his lectures; and at least three extensive and learned commentaries on it have been published within the last twenty-five years.

The difficulties of the *Timaeus* arise not from any intentional or unintentional obscurity in Plato's writing, but from the extreme compression of his exposition. It was no little achievement to bring within the scope of Timaeus' discourse, occupying about sixty-five pages of Stephanus' text, the whole, or almost the whole, of the natural science of his day. To accomplish this, Plato has to omit in most cases everything except the main outlines of his theory, leaving the rest to be supplied by his readers, who are presumed to be "familiar with those branches of learning which this exposition requires" (53c). Unfortunately, with the passage of time these branches of learning came to be superseded or forgotten, so that a competent commentary is today indispensable for the full understanding of Plato's thought.

GLENN R. MORROW

University of Pennsylvania
July, 1949.

Note on the Edition

The present edition is a reprint of the third edition of Jowett's translation. Spelling and punctuation have been revised to conform to current American usage.

To facilitate reference to passages in the dialogue the pagination of Stephanus' edition of Plato (Paris, 1578) has been used in the introduction and in the margins of the text.

Timaeus

CHARACTERS OF THE DIALOGUE

SOCRATES

TIMAEUS

CRITIAS

HERMOCRATES

Socrates. ONE, two, three; but where, my dear Timaeus, is the fourth of those who were yesterday my guests and are to be my entertainers today?

Timaeus. He has been taken ill, Socrates; for he would not willingly have been absent from this gathering.

Soc. Then, if he is not coming, you and the two others must supply his place.

Tim. Certainly, and we will do all that we can; having been handsomely entertained by you yesterday, those of us who remain should be only too glad to return your hospitality.

Soc. Do you remember what were the points of which I required you to speak?

Tim. We remember some of them, and you will be here to remind us of anything which we have forgotten; or rather, if we are not troubling you, will you briefly recapitulate the whole, and then the particulars will be more firmly fixed in our memories?

Soc. To be sure I will: the chief theme of my yesterday's discourse was the State—how constituted and of what citizens composed it would seem likely to be most perfect.

Tim. Yes, Socrates; and what you said of it was very much to our mind.

Soc. Did we not begin by separating the husbandmen and the artisans from the class of defenders of the State?

Tim. Yes.

Soc. And when we had given to each one that single employment and particular art which was suited to his nature, we spoke of those who were intended to be our warriors, and said that they were to be guardians of the city against attacks from within as well as from without, and to have no other employment; they were to be merciful in judging their subjects, of whom they were by nature friends, but fierce to their enemies, when they came across them in battle.

Tim. Exactly.

Soc. We said, if I am not mistaken, that the guardians should be gifted with a temperament in a high degree both passionate and philosophical; and that then they would be as they ought to be— gentle to their friends and fierce with their enemies.

Tim. Certainly.

Soc. And what did we say of their education? Were they not to be trained in gymnastic and music and all other sorts of knowledge which were proper for them ?[1]

Tim. Very true.

Soc. And being thus trained they were not to consider gold or silver or anything else to be their own private property; they were to be like hired troops, receiving pay for keeping guard from those who were protected by them—the pay was to be no more than would suffice for men of simple life; and they were to spend in common, and to live together in the continual practice of virtue, which was to be their sole pursuit.

Tim. That was also said.

Soc. Neither did we forget the women, of whom we declared that their natures should be assimilated and brought into harmony with those of the men, and that common pursuits should be assigned to them both in time of war and in their ordinary life.

Tim. That, again, was as you say.

Soc. And what about the procreation of children? Or rather was not the proposal too singular to be forgotten? For all wives and children were to be in common, to the intent that no one should ever know his own child, but they were to imagine that they were all one family; those who were within a suitable limit of age were to be brothers and sisters, those who were of an elder generation parents and grandparents, and those of a younger, children and grandchildren.

[1] Or 'which are akin to these'; or τούτοις may be taken with ἐν ἅπασι.

Tim. Yes, and the proposal is easy to remember, as you say.

Soc. And do you also remember how, with a view of securing as far as we could the best breed, we said that the chief magistrates, male and female, should contrive secretly, by the use of certain lots, so to arrange the nuptial meeting, that the bad of either sex and the good of either sex might pair with their like; and there was to be no quarrelling on this account, for they would imagine that the union was a mere accident and was to be attributed to the lot?

Tim. I remember.

Soc. And you remember how we said that the children of the good parents were to be educated, and the children of the bad secretly dispersed among the inferior citizens; and while they were all growing up the rulers were to be on the look-out, and to bring up from below in their turn those who were worthy, and those among themselves who were unworthy were to take the places of those who came up?

Tim. True.

Soc. Then have I now given you all the heads of our yesterday's discussion? Or is there anything more, my dear Timaeus, which has been omitted?

Tim. Nothing, Socrates; it was just as you have said.

Soc. I should like, before proceeding further, to tell you how I feel about the State which we have described. I might compare myself to a person who, on beholding beautiful animals either created by the painter's art, or, better still, alive but at rest, is seized with a desire of seeing them in motion or engaged in some struggle or conflict to which their forms appear suited; this is my feeling about the State which we have been describing. There are conflicts which all cities undergo, and I should like to hear some one tell of our own city carrying on a struggle against her neighbors, and how she went out to war in a becoming manner, and when at war showed by the greatness of her actions and the magnanimity of her words in dealing with other cities a result worthy of her training and education. Now I, Critias and Hermocrates, am conscious that I myself should never be able to celebrate the city and her citizens in a befitting manner, and I am not surprised at my own incapacity; to me the wonder is rather that the poets present as well as past are no better—not that I mean to depreciate them; but everyone can

10

see that they are a tribe of imitators, and will imitate best and most easily the life in which they have been brought up; while that which is beyond the range of a man's education he finds hard to carry out in action, and still harder adequately to represent in language. I am aware that the Sophists have plenty of brave words and fair conceits, but I am afraid that being only wanderers from one city to another, and having never had habitations of their own, they may fail in their conception of philosophers and statesmen and may not know what they do and say in time of war, when they are fighting or holding parley with their enemies. And thus people of your class are the only ones remaining who are fitted by nature and education to take part at once both in politics and philosophy.

20 Here is Timaeus, of Locris in Italy, a city which has admirable laws, and who is himself in wealth and rank the equal of any of his fellow citizens; he has held the most important and honorable offices in his own state, and, as I believe, has scaled the heights of all philosophy; and here is Critias, whom every Athenian knows to be no novice in the matters of which we are speaking; and as to Hermocrates, I am assured by many witnesses that his genius and education qualify him to take part in any speculation of the kind. And therefore yesterday when I saw that you wanted me to describe the formation of the State, I readily assented, being very well aware that, if you only would, none were better qualified to carry the discussion further, and that when you had engaged our city in a suitable war, you of all men living could best exhibit her playing a fitting part. When I had completed my task, I in return imposed this other task upon you. You conferred together and agreed to entertain me today, as I had entertained you, with a feast of discourse. Here am I in festive array, and no man can be more ready for the promised banquet.

Hermocrates. And we too, Socrates, as Timaeus says, will not be wanting in enthusiasm; and there is no excuse for not complying with your request. As soon as we arrived yesterday at the guest-chamber of Critias, with whom we are staying, or rather on our way thither, we talked the matter over, and he told us an ancient tradition which I wish, Critias, that you would repeat to Socrates, so that he may help us to judge whether it will satisfy his requirements or not.

Critias. I will, if Timaeus, who is our other partner, approves.

Tim. I quite approve.

Crit. Then listen, Socrates, to a tale which, though strange, is certainly true, having been attested by Solon, who was the wisest of the seven sages. He was a relative and a dear friend of my great-grandfather, Dropides, as he himself says in many passages of his poems; and he told the story to Critias, my grandfather, who remembered and repeated it to us. There were of old, he said, great and marvelous actions of the Athenian city, which have passed into oblivion through lapse of time and the destruction of mankind, and one in particular, greater than all the rest. This we will now rehearse. It will be a fitting monument of our gratitude to you, and a hymn of praise true and worthy of the goddess, on this her day of festival.

Soc. Very good. And what is this ancient famous action of the Athenians, which Critias declared, on the authority of Solon, to be not a mere legend but an actual fact?[2]

Crit. I will tell an old-world story which I heard from an aged man; for Critias, at the time of telling it, was, as he said, nearly ninety years of age, and I was about ten. Now the day was that day of the Apaturia which is called the Registration of Youth, at which, according to custom, our parents gave prizes for recitations, and the poems of several poets were recited by us boys, and many of us sang the poems of Solon, which at that time had not gone out of fashion. One of our tribe, either because he thought so or to please Critias, said that in his judgment Solon was not only the wisest of men, but also the noblest of poets. The old man, as I very well remember, brightened up at hearing this and said, smiling: Yes, Amynander, if Solon had only, like other poets, made poetry the business of his life and had completed the tale which he brought with him from Egypt, and had not been compelled, by reason of the factions and troubles which he found stirring in his own country when he came home, to attend to other matters, in my opinion he would have been as famous as Homer or Hesiod, or any poet.

And what was the tale about, Critias? said Amynander.

[2] Or "which, though unrecorded in history, Critias declared, on the authority of Solon, to be an actual fact?"

About the greatest action which the Athenians ever did, and which ought to have been the most famous, but, through the lapse of time and the destruction of the actors, it has not come down to us.

Tell us, said the other, the whole story, and how and from whom Solon heard this veritable tradition.

He replied: In the Egyptian Delta, at the head of which the river Nile divides, there is a certain district which is called the district of Sais, and the great city of the district is also called Sais, and is the city from which King Amasis came. The citizens have a deity for their foundress; she is called in the Egyptian tongue Neith, and is asserted by them to be the same whom the Hellenes call Athene; they are great lovers of the Athenians and say that they are in some way related to them. To this city came Solon and was received there with great honor; he asked the priests, who were most skillful in such matters, about antiquity, and made the discovery that neither he nor any other Hellene knew anything worth mentioning about the times of old. On one occasion, wishing to draw them on to speak of antiquity, he began to tell about the most ancient things in our part of the world—about Phoroneus, who is called "the first man," and about Niobe; and after the Deluge, of the survival of Deucalion and Pyrrha; and he traced the genealogy of their descendants and, reckoning up the dates, tried to compute how many years ago the events of which he was speaking happened. Thereupon one of the priests, who was of a very great age, said: O Solon, Solon, you Hellenes are never anything but children, and there is not an old man among you. Solon in return asked him what he meant. I mean to say, he replied, that in mind you are all young; there is no old opinion handed down among you by ancient tradition, nor any science which is hoary with age. And I will tell you why. There have been, and will be again, many destructions of mankind arising out of many causes; the greatest have been brought about by the agencies of fire and water, and other lesser ones by innumerable other causes. There is a story which even you have preserved, that once upon a time Phaëthon, the son of Helios, having yoked the steeds in his father's chariot, because he was not able to drive them in the path of his father, burnt up all that was upon the earth, and was himself destroyed by a thunderbolt. Now this has the form of a myth, but really signifies a declination of the bodies moving in the heavens around the earth, and a great conflagration of things upon the earth which recurs after long intervals; at such times those who live upon the mountains and in dry and lofty places are more liable to destruction than those who dwell by rivers or on the seashore. And from this calamity the Nile, who is our never-failing savior, delivers and preserves us. When, on the other hand, the gods purge the earth with a deluge of water, the survivors in your country are herdsmen and shepherds who dwell on the mountains, but those who, like you, live in cities are carried by the rivers into the sea. Whereas in this land, neither then nor at any other time, does the water come down from above on the fields, having always a tendency to come up from below; for which reason the traditions preserved here are the most ancient. The fact is that wherever the extremity of winter frost or of summer sun does not prevent, mankind exist, sometimes in greater, sometimes in lesser numbers. And whatever happened either in your country or in ours, or in any other region of which we are informed—if there were any actions noble or great or in any other way remarkable, they have all been written down by us of old and are preserved in our temples. Whereas just when you and other nations are beginning to be provided with letters and the other requisites of civilized life, after the usual interval, the stream from heaven, like a pestilence, comes pouring down and leaves only those of you who are destitute of letters and education; and so you have to begin all over again like children, and know nothing of what happened in ancient times, either among us or among yourselves. As for those genealogies of yours which you just now recounted to us, Solon, they are no better than the tales of children. In the first place you remember a single deluge only, but there were many previous ones; in the next place, you do not know that there formerly dwelt in your land the fairest and noblest race of men which ever lived, and that you and your whole city are descended from a small seed or remnant of them which survived. And this was unknown to you, because, for many generations, the survivors of that destruction died, leaving no written word. For there was a time, Solon, before the great deluge of all, when the city which now is Athens was first in war and in every way the best governed of all cities, and is said to have performed the noblest deeds and to have had the fairest constitution of any of which tradition tells, under the face of heaven. Solon marveled at his words, and earnestly requested the priests to inform him exactly and in order about these former citizens. You are welcome to hear about them, Solon, said the priest, both for your own sake and for that of your city, and above all, for the sake of the goddess who is the common patron and parent and educator of both our cities. She founded your city a thousand years before ours,[3] receiving from the Earth and Hephaestus the seed of your race; and afterwards she founded ours, of which the constitution is recorded in our sacred registers to be 8000 years old. As touching your citizens of 9000 years ago, I will briefly inform you of their laws and of their most famous action; the exact particulars of the whole we will hereafter go through at our leisure in the sacred registers themselves. If you compare these very laws with ours you will find that many of ours are the counterpart of yours as they were in the olden time. In the first place, there is the caste of priests, which is separated from all the others; next, there are the artificers, who ply their several crafts by themselves and do not intermix; and also there is the class of shepherds and of hunters,[4] as well as that of husbandmen; and you will observe, too, that the warriors in Egypt are distinct from all the other classes, and are commanded by the law to devote themselves solely to military pursuits; moreover, the weapons which they carry are shields and spears—a style of equipment which the goddess taught of Asiatics first to us, as in your part of the world first to you. Then as to wisdom, do you observe how our law from the very first made a study of the whole order of things, extending even to prophecy and medicine which gives health, out of these divine elements deriving what was needful for human life, and adding every sort of knowledge which was akin to them. All this order and arrangement the goddess first imparted to you when establishing your city; and she chose the spot of earth in which you were born, because she saw that the happy temperament of the seasons in that land would produce the wisest of men. Wherefore the god-

---

[3] Observe that Plato gives the same date (9000 years ago) for the foundation of Athens and for the repulse of the invasion from Atlantis (Crit. 108e).

[4] Reading τὸ τῶν θηρευτῶν.

dess, who was a lover both of war and of wisdom, selected and first of all settled that spot which was the most likely to produce men likest herself. And there you dwelt, having such laws as these and still better ones, and excelled all mankind in all virtue, as became the children and disciples of the gods.

Many great and wonderful deeds are recorded of your state in our histories. But one of them exceeds all the rest in greatness and valor. For these histories tell of a mighty power which unprovoked made an expedition against the whole of Europe and Asia, and to which your city put an end. This power came forth out of the Atlantic Ocean, for in those days the Atlantic was navigable; and there was an island situated in front of the straits which are by you called the pillars of Heracles; the island was larger than Libya and Asia put together, and was the way to other islands, and from these you might pass to the whole of the opposite continent which surrounded the true ocean; for this sea which is within the Straits of Heracles is only a harbor, having a narrow entrance, but that other is a real sea, and the surrounding land may be most truly called a boundless continent. Now in this island of Atlantis there was a great and wonderful empire which had rule over the whole island and several others, and over parts of the continent, and, furthermore, the men of Atlantis had subjected the parts of Libya within the columns of Heracles as far as Egypt, and of Europe as far as Tyrrhenia. This vast power, gathered into one, endeavored to subdue at a blow our country and yours and the whole of the region within the straits; and then, Solon, your country shone forth, in the excellence of her virtue and strength, among all mankind. She was pre-eminent in courage and military skill, and was the leader of the Hellenes. And when the rest fell off from her, being compelled to stand alone, after having undergone the very extremity of danger, she defeated and triumphed over the invaders, and preserved from slavery those who were not yet subjugated, and generously liberated all the rest of us who dwell within the pillars. But afterwards there occurred violent earthquakes and floods; and in a single day and night of misfortune all your warlike men in a body sank into the earth, and the island of Atlantis in like manner disappeared in the depths of the sea. For which reason the sea in those parts is impassable and impenetrable, because there is a shoal of mud in the way; and this was caused by the subsidence of the island.

I have told you briefly, Socrates, what the aged Critias heard from Solon and related to us. And when you were speaking yesterday about your city and citizens, the tale which I have just been repeating to you came into my mind, and I remarked with astonishment how, by some mysterious coincidence, you agreed in almost every particular with the narrative of Solon; but I did not like to speak at the moment. For a long time had elapsed, and I had forgotten too much; I thought that I must first of all run over the narrative in my own mind, and then I would speak. And so I readily assented to your request yesterday, considering that in all such cases the chief difficulty is to find a tale suitable to our purpose, and that with such a tale we should be fairly well provided.

And therefore, as Hermocrates has told you, on my way home yesterday I at once communicated the tale to my companions as I remembered it; and after I left them, during the night by thinking I recovered nearly the whole of it. Truly, as is often said, the lessons of our childhood make a wonderful impression on our memories; for I am not sure that I could remember all the discourse of yesterday, but I should be much surprised if I forgot any of these things which I have heard very long ago. I listened at the time with childlike interest to the old man's narrative; he was very ready to teach me, and I asked him again and again to repeat his words, so that, like an indelible picture, they were branded into my mind. As soon as the day broke, I rehearsed them as he spoke them to my companions, that they, as well as myself, might have something to say. And now, Socrates, to make an end of my preface, I am ready to tell you the whole tale. I will give you not only the general heads, but the particulars, as they were told to me. The city and citizens, which you yesterday described to us in fiction, we will now transfer to the world of reality. It shall be the ancient city of Athens, and we will suppose that the citizens whom you imagined were our veritable ancestors of whom the priest spoke; they will perfectly harmonize, and there will be no inconsistency in saying that the citizens of your republic are these ancient Athenians. Let us divide the subject among us, and all endeavor according to our ability gracefully to execute the task which you have imposed upon us. Consider then, Socrates, if this narrative is suited to the purpose, or whether we should seek for some other instead.

Soc. And what other, Critias, can we find that will be better than this which is natural and suitable to the festival of the goddess, and has the very great advantage of being a fact and not a fiction? How or where shall we find another if we abandon this? We cannot, and therefore you must tell the tale, and good luck to you; and I in return for my yesterday's discourse will now rest and be a listener.

Crit. Let me proceed to explain to you, Socrates, the order in which we have arranged our entertainment. Our intention is that Timaeus, who is the most of an astronomer among us, and has made the nature of the universe his special study, should speak first, beginning with the generation of the world and going down to the creation of man; next, I am to receive the men whom he has created of whom some will have profited by the excellent education which you have given them; and then, in accordance with the tale of Solon, and equally with his law, we will bring them into court and make them citizens, as if they were those very Athenians whom the sacred Egyptian record has recovered from oblivion, and thenceforward we will speak of them as Athenians and fellow citizens.

Soc. I see that I shall receive in my turn a perfect and splendid feast of reason. And now, Timaeus, you, I suppose, should speak next, after duly calling upon the Gods.

Tim. All men, Socrates, who have any degree of right feeling, at the beginning of every enterprise, whether small or great, always call upon God. And we, too, who are going to discourse of the nature of the universe, how created or how existing without creation, if we be not altogether out of our wits, must invoke the aid of Gods and Goddesses and pray that our words may be acceptable to them and consistent with themselves. Let this, then, be our invocation of the Gods, to which I add an exhortation of myself to speak in such manner as will be most intelligible to you, and will most accord with my own intent.

First then, in my judgment, we must make a distinction and ask, What is that which always is and has no becoming; and what is that which is always becoming and never is? That which is appre-

28 hended by intelligence and reason is always in the same state; but that which is conceived by opinion with the help of sensation and without reason, is always in a process of becoming and perishing and never really is. Now everything that becomes or is created[5] must of necessity be created by some cause, for without a cause nothing can be created. The work of the creator, whenever he looks to the unchangeable and fashions the form and nature of his work after an unchangeable pattern, must necessarily be made fair and perfect; but when he looks to the created only and uses a created pattern, it is not fair or perfect. Was the heaven then or the world, whether called by this or by any other more appropriate name— assuming the name, I am asking a question which has to be asked at the beginning of an inquiry about anything—was the world, I say, always in existence and without beginning, or created, and had it a beginning? Created, I reply, being visible and tangible and having a body, and therefore sensible; and all sensible things are apprehended by opinion and sense, and are in a process of creation and created. Now that which is created must, as we affirm, of necessity be created by a cause. But the father and maker of all this universe is past finding out;[6] and even if we found him, to tell of him to all men would be impossible. And there is still a question to be asked about him: Which of the patterns had the artificer in view when he made the world—the pattern of the unchangeable 29 or of that which is created? If the world be indeed fair and the artificer good, it is manifest that he must have looked to that which is eternal; but if what cannot be said without blasphemy is true, then to the created pattern. Everyone will see that he must have looked to the eternal; for the world is the fairest of creations and he is the best of causes. And having been created in this way, the world has been framed in the likeness of that which is apprehended by reason and mind and is unchangeable, and must therefore of necessity, if this is admitted, be a copy of something. Now it is all-important that the beginning of everything should be according to nature. And in speaking of the copy and the original we may as-

[5] [Jowett has a fondness for rendering γένεσις and cognate terms by "creation," "created," "creator," and the like. Γένεσις means "generation" or "coming-into-being."—Ed.]

[6] [Jowett's rendering is extreme. Plato says only that the "maker and father" is "hard to find out," not beyond our comprehension.—Ed.]

sume that words are akin to the matter which they describe; when they relate to the lasting and permanent and intelligible, they ought to be lasting and unalterable, and, as far as their nature allows, irrefutable and immovable—nothing less. But when they express only the copy or likeness and not the eternal things themselves, they need only be likely and analogous to the real words. As being is to becoming, so is truth to belief. If then, Socrates, amid the many opinions about the gods and the generation of the universe, we are not able to give notions which are altogether and in every respect exact and consistent with one another, do not be surprised. Enough if we adduce probabilities as likely as any others; for we must remember that I who am the speaker and you who are the judges are only mortal men, and we ought to accept the tale which is probable and inquire no further.

Soc. Excellent, Timaeus; and we will do precisely as you bid us. The prelude is charming and is already accepted by us—may we beg of you to proceed to the strain?

Tim. Let me tell you then why the Creator made this world of generation. He was good, and the good can never have any jealousy of anything. And being free from jealousy, he desired that all things should be as like himself as they could be. This is in the truest sense the origin of creation and of the world, as we shall do well in believing on the testimony of wise men: God desired that all things should be good and nothing bad, so far as this was attainable. Wherefore also finding the whole visible sphere[7] not at rest, but moving in an irregular and disorderly fashion, out of disorder he brought order, considering that this was in every way better than the other. Now the deeds of the best could never be or have been other than the fairest; and the Creator, reflecting on the things which are by nature visible, found that no unintelligent creature[8] taken as a whole was fairer than the intelligent taken as a whole; and that intelligence could not be present in anything

30

[7] [A more exact rendering would be, "the whole of what was visible." The spherical shape is the work of the Demiurge, and to introduce it here is premature.—*Ed.*]

[8] ["Creature" here stands for the Greek ἔργον, "work," which contains no suggestion of "living being," as the English "creature" now does. It is true that in order to put intelligence into his ἔργον, the creator has to make it a living being; but Jowett's translation puts the conclusion of the creator's reasoning into his premise.—*Ed.*]

which was devoid of soul. For which reason, when he was framing the universe, he put intelligence in soul, and soul in body, that he might be the creator of a work which was by nature fairest and best. Wherefore, using the language of probability, we may say that the world became a living creature truly endowed with soul and intelligence by the providence of God.

This being supposed, let us proceed to the next stage: In the likeness of what animal did the Creator make the world? It would be an unworthy thing to liken it to any nature which exists as a part only; for nothing can be beautiful which is like any imperfect thing: but let us suppose the world to be the very image of that whole of which all other animals both individually and in their tribes are portions. For the original of the universe contains in itself all intelligible beings, just as this world comprehends us and all other visible creatures. For the Deity, intending to make this world like the fairest and most perfect of intelligible beings, framed one visible animal comprehending within itself all other animals of a kindred nature. Are we right in saying that there is one world, or that they are many and infinite? There must be one only if the created copy is to accord with the original. For that which includes all other intelligible creatures cannot have a second or companion; in that case there would be need of another living being which would include both, and of which they would be parts, and the likeness would be more truly said to resemble not them, but that other which included them. In order then that the world might be solitary, like the perfect animal, the creator made not two worlds or an infinite number of them; but there is and ever will be one only-begotten and created heaven.[9]

Now that which is created is of necessity corporeal, and also visible and tangible. And nothing is visible where there is no fire, or tangible which has no solidity, and nothing is solid without earth. Wherefore also God in the beginning of creation made the body of the universe to consist of fire and earth. But two things

[9] [Μονογενής here rendered by "only-begotten," could also be translated "single in its kind." The second meaning is required by the reasoning of this paragraph, but no doubt both meanings were present in Plato's thought. The same phrase is used at the very end of the *Timaeus* (92c), with a similar double meaning.—*Ed.*]

cannot be rightly put together without a third; there must be some bond of union between them. And the fairest bond is that which makes the most complete fusion of itself and the things which it combines; and proportion is best adapted to effect such a union. For whenever in any three numbers, whether cube or square, there is a mean, which is to the last term what the first term is to it; and again, when the mean is to the first term as the last term is to the mean—then the mean becoming first and last, and the first and last both becoming means, they will all of them of necessity come to be the same, and having become the same with one another will be all one. If the universal frame had been created a surface only and having no depth, a single mean would have sufficed to bind together itself and the other terms; but now, as the world must be solid, and solid bodies are always compacted not by one mean but by two, God placed water and air in the mean between fire and earth, and made them to have the same proportion so far as was possible (as fire is to air so is air to water, and as air is to water so is water to earth); and thus he bound and put together a visible and tangible heaven. And for these reasons, and out of such elements which are in number four, the body of the world was created, and it was harmonized by proportion, and therefore has the spirit of friendship; and having been reconciled to itself, it was indissoluble by the hand of any other than the framer.

Now the creation took up the whole of each of the four elements; for the Creator compounded the world out of all the fire and all the water and all the air and all the earth, leaving no part of any of them nor any power of them outside. His intention was, in the first place, that the animal should be as far as possible a perfect whole and of perfect parts: secondly, that it should be one, leaving no remnants out of which another such world might be created; and also that it should be free from old age and unaffected by disease. Considering that if heat and cold and other powerful forces which unite bodies surround and attack them from without when they are unprepared, they decompose them, and by bringing diseases and old age upon them make them waste away—for this cause and on these grounds he made the world one whole, having every part entire, and being therefore perfect and not liable to old age and disease. And he gave to the world the figure which was suitable and also natural. Now to the animal which was to comprehend all animals, that figure was suitable which comprehends within itself all other figures. Wherefore he made the world in the form of a globe, round as from a lathe, having its extremes in every direction equidistant from the center, the most perfect and the most like itself of all figures; for he considered that the like is infinitely fairer than the unlike. This he finished off, making the surface smooth all around for many reasons: in the first place, because the living being had no need of eyes when there was nothing remaining outside him to be seen, nor of ears when there was nothing to be heard; and there was no surrounding atmosphere to be breathed; nor would there have been any use of organs by the help of which he might receive his food or get rid of what he had already digested since there was nothing which went from him or came into him; for there was nothing beside him. Of design he was created thus— his own waste providing his own food, and all that he did or suffered taking place in and by himself. For the Creator conceived that a being which was self-sufficient would be far more excellent than one which lacked anything; and, as he had no need to take anything or defend himself against any one, the Creator did not think it necessary to bestow upon him hands; nor had he any need of feet, nor of the whole apparatus of walking; but the movement suited to his spherical form was assigned to him, being of all the seven that which is most appropriate to mind and intelligence; and he was made to move in the same manner and on the same spot, within his own limits revolving in a circle. All the other six motions[10] were taken away from him, and he was made not to partake of their deviations. And as this circular movement required no feet, the universe was created without legs and without feet.

Such was the whole plan of the eternal God about the god that was to be, to whom for this reason he gave a body, smooth and even, having a surface in every direction equidistant from the center, a body entire and perfect, and formed out of perfect bodies. And in the center he put the soul, which he diffused throughout the body, making it also to be the exterior environment of it; and he made the universe a circle moving in a circle, one and solitary, yet

[10] [That is, the rectilinear motions in three-dimensional space: up, down. to the right, to the left, forward, backward.—*Ed.*]

by reason of its excellence able to converse with itself, and needing no other friendship or acquaintance. Having these purposes in view he created the world a blessed god.

Now God did not make the soul after the body, although we are speaking of them in this order; for having brought them together he would never have allowed that the elder should be ruled by the younger; but this is a random manner of speaking which we have, because somehow we ourselves too are very much under the dominion of chance. Whereas he made the soul in origin and excellence prior to and older than the body, to be the ruler and mistress, of whom the body was to be the subject. And he made her out of the following elements and on this wise: Out of the indivisible and un-   35
changeable, and also out of that which is divisible and has to do with material bodies, he compounded a third and intermediate kind of essence partaking of the nature of the same[11] and of the other; and this compound he placed accordingly in a mean between the indivisible and the divisible and material. He took the three elements of the same, the other, and the essence,[12] and mingled them into one form, compressing by force the reluctant and unsociable nature of the other into the same. When he had mingled them with the essence and out of three made one, he again divided this whole into as many portions as was fitting, each portion being a compound of the same, the other, and the essence. And he proceeded to divide after this manner: First of all, he took away one part of the whole [1], and then he separated a second part which was double the first [2], and then he took away a third part which was half as much again as the second and three times as much as the first [3], and then he took a fourth part which was twice as much as the second [4], and a fifth part which was three times the third [9], and a sixth part which was eight times the first [8], and a seventh part which was twenty-seven times the first [27]. After this he filled up the double intervals [that is, between 1, 2, 4, 8]   36
and the triple [that is, between 1, 3, 9, 27], cutting off yet other portions from the mixture and placing them in the intervals, so that in each interval there were two kinds of means, the one exceeding and exceeded by equal parts of its extremes [as for example, 1, 3̇, 2,

[11] Omitting αὖ πέρι.

[12] [On this difficult passage see the Introduction, p. xviii.—Ed.]

in which the mean $\frac{4}{3}$ is one-third of 1 more than 1, and one-third of 2 less than 2], the other being that kind of mean which exceeds and is exceeded by an equal number.[13] Where there were intervals of $\frac{3}{2}$ and of $\frac{4}{3}$ and of $\frac{9}{8}$, made by the connecting terms in the former intervals, he filled up all the intervals of $\frac{4}{3}$ with the interval of $\frac{9}{8}$, leaving a fraction over; and the interval which this fraction expressed was in the ratio of 256 to 243.[14] And thus the whole mixture out of which he cut these portions was all exhausted by him. This entire compound he divided lengthways into two parts which he joined to one another at the center like the letter X, and bent them into a circular form, connecting them with themselves and each other at the point opposite to their original meeting point; and, comprehending them in a uniform revolution upon the same axis, he made the one the outer and the other the inner circle. Now the motion of the outer circle he called the motion of the same, and the motion of the inner circle the motion of the other or diverse. The motion of the same he carried round by the side[15] to the right, and the motion of the diverse diagonally[16] to the left. And he gave dominion to the ...:otion of the same and like, for that he left single and undivided; but the inner motion he divided in six places and made seven unequal circles having their intervals in ratios of two and three, three of each, and bade the orbits proceed in a direction opposite to one another; and three [Sun, Mercury, Venus] he made to move with equal swiftness, and the remaining four [Moon, Saturn, Mars, Jupiter] to move with unequal swiftness to the three and to one another, but in due proportion.

Now when the Creator had framed the soul according to his will, he formed within her the corporeal universe, and brought the two together and united them center to center. The soul, interfused everywhere from the center to the circumference of heaven of which also she is the external envelopment, herself turning in her-

[13] For example, $\overline{1}, \frac{4}{3}, \frac{3}{2}, \overline{2}, \frac{5}{3}, 3, 4, \frac{16}{3}, 6, \overline{8}$; and

$\overline{1}, \frac{3}{2}, 2, \overline{3}, \frac{9}{2}, 6, 9, \overline{\frac{27}{2}}, 18, \overline{27}$.

[14] For example, $243 : 256 :: \frac{81}{64} : \frac{4}{3} :: \frac{243}{128} : 2 :: \frac{81}{32} : \frac{8}{3} :: \frac{243}{64} : 4 :: \frac{81}{16} : \frac{16}{3} :: \frac{243}{32} : 8$.

(MARTIN.)

[15] That is, of the rectangular figure supposed to be inscribed in the circle of the Same.

[16] That is, across the rectangular figure from corner to corner.

self, began a divine beginning of never-ceasing and rational life enduring throughout all time. The body of heaven is visible, but the soul is invisible and partakes of reason and harmony, and, being made by the best of intellectual and everlasting natures, is the best of things created. And because she is composed of the same and of the other and of the essence—these three—and is divided and united in due proportion, and in her revolutions returns upon herself, the soul, when touching anything which has essence, whether dispersed in parts or undivided, is stirred through all her powers to declare the sameness or difference of that thing and some other, and to what individuals are related, and by what affected, and in what way and how and when, both in the world of generation and in the world of immutable being. And when reason, which works with equal truth, whether she be in the circle of the diverse or of the same—in voiceless silence holding her onward course in the sphere of the self-moved—when reason, I say, is hovering around the sensible world and when the circle of the diverse also moving truly imparts the intimations of sense to the whole soul, then arise opinions and beliefs sure and certain. But when reason is concerned with the rational, and the circle of the same moving smoothly declares it, then intelligence and knowledge are necessarily perfected. And if any one affirms that in which these two are found to be other than the soul, he will say the very opposite of the truth.

When the Father and Creator saw the creature which he had made moving and living, the created image of the eternal gods, he rejoiced, and in his joy determined to make the copy still more like the original; and as this was eternal, he sought to make the universe eternal, so far as might be. Now the nature of the ideal being was everlasting, but to bestow this attribute in its fullness upon a creature was impossible. Wherefore he resolved to have a moving image of eternity, and when he set in order the heaven, he made this image eternal but moving according to number, while eternity itself rests in unity; and this image we call time. For there were no days and nights and months and years before the heaven was created, but when he constructed the heaven he created them also. They are all parts of time, and the past and future are created species of time, which we unconsciously but wrongly transfer to the eternal essence; for we say that he "was," he "is," he "will be,"

but the truth is that "is" alone is properly attributed to him, and that "was" and "will be" are only to be spoken of becoming in time, for they are motions, but that which is immovably the same cannot become older or younger by time, nor ever did or has become, or hereafter will be, older or younger, nor is subject at all to any of those states which affect moving and sensible things and of which generation is the cause. These are the forms of time, which imitates eternity and revolves according to a law of number. Moreover, when we say that what has become *is* become and what becomes *is* becoming, and that what will become *is* about to become and that the non-existent *is* non-existent—all these are inaccurate modes of expression.[17] But perhaps this whole subject will be more suitably discussed on some other occasion.

Time, then, and the heaven came into being at the same instant in order that, having been created together, if ever there was to be a dissolution of them, they might be dissolved together. It was framed after the pattern of the eternal nature—that it might resemble this as far as was possible; for the pattern exists from eternity, and the created heaven has been and is and will be in all time. Such was the mind and thought of God in the creation of time. The sun and moon and five other stars, which are called the planets, were created by him in order to distinguish and preserve the numbers of time; and when he had made their several bodies, he placed them in the orbits in which the circle of the other was revolving (cp. 36d)—in seven orbits seven stars. First, there was the moon in the orbit nearest the earth; and next the sun, in the second orbit above the earth; then came the morning star and the star sacred to Hermes, moving in orbits which have an equal swiftness with the sun, but in an opposite direction; and this is the reason why the sun and Hermes and Lucifer overtake and are overtaken by each other. To enumerate the places which he assigned to the other stars and to give all the reasons why he assigned them, although a secondary matter, would give more trouble than the primary. These things at some future time, when we are at leisure, may have the consideration which they deserve, but not at present.

[17] Cp. Parmen. 141.

Now, when all the stars which were necessary to the creation of time had attained a motion suitable to them, and had become living creatures having bodies fastened by vital chains, and learned their appointed task—moving in the motion of the diverse, which is diagonal and passes through and is governed by the motion of the same—they revolved, some in a larger and some in a lesser orbit: those which had the lesser orbit revolving faster, and those which had the larger more slowly. Now by reason of the motion of the same, those which revolved fastest appeared to be overtaken by those which moved slower although they really overtook them; for the motion of the same made them all turn in a spiral, and, because some went one way and some another, that which receded most slowly from the sphere of the same, which was the swiftest, appeared to follow it most nearly. That there might be some visible measure of their relative swiftness and slowness as they proceeded in their eight courses, God lighted a fire, which we now call the sun, in the second from the earth of these orbits, that it might give light to the whole of heaven, and that the animals, as many as nature intended, might participate in number, learning arithmetic from the revolution of the same and the like. Thus, then, and for this reason the night and the day were created, being the period of the one most intelligent revolution. And the month is accomplished when the moon has completed her orbit and overtaken the sun, and the year when the sun has completed his own orbit. Mankind, with hardly an exception, have not remarked the periods of the other stars, and they have no name for them, and do not measure them against one another by the help of number, and hence they can scarcely be said to know that their wanderings, being infinite in number and admirable for their variety, make up time. And yet there is no difficulty in seeing that the perfect number of time fulfills the perfect year when all the eight revolutions, having their relative degrees of swiftness, are accomplished together and attain their completion at the same time, measured by the rotation of the same and equally moving. After this manner, and for these reasons, came into being such of the stars as in their heavenly progress received reversals of motion, to the end that the created heaven might imitate the eternal nature, and be as like as possible to the perfect and intelligible animal.

Thus far and until the birth of time the created universe was made in the likeness of the original, but inasmuch as all animals were not yet comprehended therein, it was still unlike. What remained, the Creator then proceeded to fashion after the nature of the pattern. Now as in the ideal animal the mind perceives ideas or species of a certain nature and number, he thought that this created animal ought to have species of a like nature and number. There are four such: one of them is the heavenly race of the gods; another, the race of birds whose way is in the air; the third, the watery species; and the fourth, the pedestrian and land creatures. Of the heavenly and divine, he created the greater part out of fire, that they might be the brightest of all things and fairest to behold, and he fashioned them after the likeness of the universe in the figure of a circle, and made them follow the intelligent motion of the supreme, distributing them over the whole circumference of heaven, which was to be a true cosmos or glorious world spangled with them all over. And he gave to each of them two movements: the first, a movement on the same spot after the same manner, whereby they ever continue to think consistently the same thoughts about the same things; the second, a forward movement, in which they are controlled by the revolution of the same and the like; but by the other five motions they were unaffected (cp. 43b), in order that each of them might attain the highest perfection. And for this reason the fixed stars were created, to be divine and eternal animals, ever-abiding and revolving after the same manner and on the same spot; and the other stars which reverse their motion and are subject to deviations of this kind were created in the manner already described. The earth, which is our nurse, clinging[18] around the pole which is extended through the universe, he framed to be the guardian and artificer of night and day, first and eldest of gods that are in the interior of heaven. Vain would be the attempt to tell all the figures of them circling as in dance, and their juxtapositions, and the return of them in their revolutions upon themselves, and their approximations, and to say which of these deities in their conjunctions meet, and which of them are in opposition, and in what order they get behind and before one another, and when they are severally eclipsed to our sight and again reappear, sending

[18] Or "circling."

terrors and intimations of the future to those who cannot calculate their movements—to attempt to tell of all this without a visible representation of the heavenly system[19] would be labor in vain. Enough on this head; and now let what we have said about the nature of the created and visible gods have an end.

To know or tell the origin of the other divinities is beyond us, and we must accept the traditions of the men of old time who affirm themselves to be the offspring of the gods—that is what they say—and they must surely have known their own ancestors. How can we doubt the word of the children of the gods? Although they give no probable or certain proofs, still, as they declare that they are speaking of what took place in their own family, we must conform to custom and believe them. In this manner, then, according to them, the genealogy of these gods is to be received and set forth.

Oceanus and Tethys were the children of Earth and Heaven, and from these sprang Phorcys and Cronos and Rhea, and all that generation; and from Cronos and Rhea sprang Zeus and Herè, and all those who are said to be their brethren, and others who were the children of these.

41

Now, when all of them, both those who visibly appear in their revolutions as well as those other gods who are of a more retiring nature, had come into being, the creator of the universe addressed them in these words: "Gods, children of gods, who are my works and of whom I am the artificer and father, my creations are indissoluble, if so I will. All that is bound may be undone, but only an evil being would wish to undo that which is harmonious and happy. Wherefore, since ye are but creatures, ye are not altogether immortal and indissoluble, but ye shall certainly not be dissolved, nor be liable to the fate of death, having in my will a greater and mightier bond than those with which ye were bound at the time of your birth. And now listen to my instructions: Three tribes of mortal beings remain to be created—without them the universe will be incomplete, for it will not contain every kind of animal which it ought to contain, if it is to be perfect. On the other hand, if they were created by me and received life at my hands, they would be on an equality with the gods. In order then that they may be mortal, and that this universe may be truly universal, do

[19] Reading τοῖς οὐ ὄυν. and τούτων αὐτῶν.

ye, according to your natures, betake yourselves to the formation of animals, imitating the power which was shown by me in creating you. The part of them worthy of the name immortal, which is called divine and is the guiding principle of those who are willing to follow justice and you—of that divine part I will myself sow the seed, and having made a beginning, I will hand the work over to you. And do ye then interweave the mortal with the immortal and make and beget living creatures, and give them food and make them to grow, and receive them again in death."

Thus he spake, and once more into the cup in which he had previously mingled the soul of the universe he poured the remains of the elements, and mingled them in much the same manner; they were not, however, pure as before, but diluted to the second and third degree. And having made it he divided the whole mixture into souls equal in number to the stars and assigned each soul to a star; and having there placed them as in a chariot he showed them the nature of the universe and declared to them the laws of destiny, according to which their first birth would be one and the same for all—no one should suffer a disadvantage at his hands; they were to be sown in the instruments of time severally adapted to them, and to come forth the most religious of animals; and as human nature was of two kinds, the superior race would hereafter be called man. Now, when they should be implanted in bodies by necessity and be always gaining or losing some part of their bodily substance, then, in the first place, it would be necessary that they should all have in them one and the same faculty of sensation, arising out of irresistible impressions; in the second place, they must have love, in which pleasure and pain mingle; also fear and anger, and the feelings which are akin or opposite to them; if they conquered these they would live righteously, and if they were conquered by them, unrighteously. He who lived well during his appointed time was to return and dwell in his native star, and there he would have a blessed and congenial existence. But if he failed in attaining this, at the second birth he would pass into a woman, and if, when in that state of being, he did not desist from evil, he would continually be changed into some brute who resembled him in the evil nature which he had acquired, and would not cease from his toils and transformations until he followed the

42

revolution of the same and the like within him, and overcame by the help of reason the turbulent and irrational mob of later accretions made up of fire and air and water and earth, and returned to the form of his first and better state. Having given all these laws to his creatures, that he might be guiltless of future evil in any of them, the creator sowed some of them in the earth, and some in the moon, and some in the other instruments of time; and when he had sown them he committed to the younger gods the fashioning of their mortal bodies, and desired them to furnish what was still lacking to the human soul, and having made all the suitable additions, to rule over them, and to pilot the mortal animal in the best and wisest manner which they could and avert from him all but self-inflicted evils.

When the creator had made all these ordinances he remained in his own accustomed nature, and his children heard and were obedient to their father's word, and receiving from him the immortal principle of a mortal creature, in imitation of their own creator they borrowed portions of fire and earth and water and air from the world, which were hereafter to be restored—these they took and welded them together, not with the indissoluble chains by which they were themselves bound, but with little pegs too small to be visible, making up out of all the four elements each separate body, and fastening the courses of the immortal soul in a body which was in a state of perpetual influx and efflux. Now these courses, detained as in a vast river, neither overcame nor were overcome, but were hurrying and hurried to and fro, so that the whole animal was moved and progressed, irregularly however and irrationally and anyhow, in all the six directions of motion, wandering backwards and forwards, and right and left, and up and down, and in all the six directions. For great as was the advancing and retiring flood which provided nourishment, the affections produced by external contact caused still greater tumult—when the body of any one met and came into collision with some external fire or with the solid earth or the gliding waters, or was caught in the tempest borne on the air—and the motions produced by any of these impulses were carried through the body to the soul. All such motions have consequently received the general name of "sensations," which they still retain. And they did in fact at that time create a

43

very great and mighty movement; uniting with the everflowing stream in stirring up and violently shaking the courses of the soul, they completely stopped the revolution of the same by their opposing current and hindered it from predominating and advancing; and they so disturbed the nature of the other or diverse that the three double intervals [that is, between 1, 2, 4, 8], and the three triple intervals [that is, between 1, 3, 9, 27], together with the mean terms and connecting links which are expressed by the ratios of 3 : 2, and 4 : 3, and of 9 : 8—these, although they cannot be wholly undone except by him who united them, were twisted by them in all sorts of ways, and the circles were broken and disordered in every possible manner, so that when they moved they were tumbling to pieces and moved irrationally, at one time in a reverse direction, and then again obliquely, and then upside down, as you might imagine a person who is upside down and has his head leaning upon the ground and his feet up against something in the air; and when he is in such a position, both he and the spectator fancy that the right of either is his left, and left right. If, when powerfully experiencing these and similar effects, the revolutions of the soul come in contact with some external thing, either of the class of the same or of the other, they speak of the same or of the other in a manner the very opposite of the truth; and they become false and foolish, and there is no course or revolution in them which has a guiding or directing power; and if again any sensations enter in violently from without and drag after them the whole vessel of the soul, then the courses of the soul, though they seem to conquer, are really conquered.

And by reason of all these affections, the soul, when encased in a mortal body, now, as in the beginning, is at first without intelligence; but when the flood of growth and nutriment abates and the courses of the soul, calming down, go their own way and become steadier as time goes on, then the several circles return to their natural form and their revolutions are corrected, and they call the same and the other by their right names and make the possessor of them to become a rational being. And if these combine in him with any true nurture or education, he attains the fullness and health of the perfect man, and escapes the worst disease of all; but if he neglects education he walks lame to the end of his life and returns imperfect and good for nothing to the world below. This, however, is a later stage; at present we must treat more exactly the subject before us, which involves a preliminary inquiry into the generation of the body and its members, and as to how the soul was created—for what reason and by what providence of the gods; and holding fast to probability we must pursue our way.

First, then, the gods, imitating the spherical shape of the universe, enclosed the two divine courses in a spherical body, that, namely, which we now term the head, being the most divine part of us and the lord of all that is in us; to this the gods, when they put together the body, gave all the other members to be servants, considering that it partook of every sort of motion. In order then that it might not tumble about among the high and deep places of the earth, but might be able to get over the one and out of the other, they provided the body to be its vehicle and means of locomotion; which consequently had length and was furnished with four limbs extended and flexible; these God contrived to be instruments of locomotion with which it might take hold and find support, and so be able to pass through all places, carrying on high the dwelling-place of the most sacred and divine part of us. Such was the origin of legs and hands, which for this reason were attached to every man; and the gods, deeming the front part of man to be more honorable and more fit to command than the hinder part, made us to move mostly in a forward direction. Wherefore man must needs have his front part unlike and distinguished from the rest of his body. And so in the vessel of the head, they first of all put a face in which they inserted organs to minister in all things to the providence of the soul, and they appointed this part, which has authority, to be by nature the part which is in front. And of the organs they first contrived the eyes to give light; and the principle according to which they were inserted was as follows: so much of fire as would not burn, but gave a gentle light, they formed into a substance akin to the light of everyday life; and the pure fire which is within us and related thereto they made to flow through the eyes in a stream smooth and dense, compressing the whole eye and especially the center part, so that it kept out everything of a coarser nature and allowed to pass only this pure element. When the light of day surrounds the stream of vision, then

45

like falls upon like, and they coalesce, and one body is formed by natural affinity in the line of vision, wherever the light that falls from within meets with an external object. And the whole stream of vision, being similarly affected in virtue of similarity, diffuses the motions of what it touches or what touches it over the whole body, until they reach the soul, causing that perception which we call sight. But when night comes on and the external and kindred fire departs, then the stream of vision is cut off; for going forth to an unlike element it is changed and extinguished, being no longer of one nature with the surrounding atmosphere which is now deprived of fire; and so the eye no longer sees, and we feel disposed to sleep. For when the eyelids, which the gods invented for the preservation of sight, are closed, they keep in the internal fire; and the power of the fire diffuses and equalizes the inward motions; when they are equalized, there is rest, and when the rest is profound, sleep comes over us scarce disturbed by dreams; but where the greater motions still remain, of whatever nature and in whatever locality, they engender corresponding visions in dreams, which are remembered by us when we are awake and in the external world. And now there is no longer any difficulty in understanding the creation of images in mirrors and all smooth and bright surfaces. For from the communion of the internal and external fires, and again from the union of them and their numerous transformations when they meet in the mirror, all these appearances of necessity arise when the fire from the face coalesces with the fire from the eye on the bright and smooth surface. And right appears left and left right, because the visual rays come into contact with the rays emitted by the object in a manner contrary to the usual mode of meeting; but the right appears right, and the left left, when the position of one of the two concurring lights is reversed; and this happens when the mirror is concave and its smooth surface repels the right stream of vision to the left side, and the left to the right.[20] Or if the mirror be turned vertically, then the concavity makes the countenance appear to be all upside down, and the lower rays are driven upward and the upper downward.

[20] He is speaking of two kinds of mirrors, first the plane, secondly the concave; and the latter is supposed to be placed, first, horizontally, and then vertically.

All these are to be reckoned among the second and co-operative causes which God, carrying into execution the idea of the best as far as possible, uses as his ministers. They are thought by most men not to be the second, but the prime causes of all things, because they freeze and heat, and contract and dilate, and the like. But they are not so, for they are incapable of reason or intellect; the only being which can properly have mind is the invisible soul, whereas fire and water, and earth and air, are all of them visible bodies. The lover of intellect and knowledge ought to explore causes of intelligent nature first of all, and, secondly, of those things which, being moved by others, are compelled to move others. And this is what we too must do. Both kinds of causes should be acknowledged by us, but a distinction should be made between those which are endowed with mind and are the workers of things fair and good, and those which are deprived of intelligence and always produce chance effects without order or design. Of the second or co-operative causes of sight, which help to give to the eyes the power which they now possess, enough has been said. I will therefore now proceed to speak of the higher use and purpose for which God has given them to us. The sight in my opinion is the 47 source of the greatest benefit to us, for had we never seen the stars and the sun and the heaven, none of the words which we have spoken about the universe would ever have been uttered. But now the sight of day and night, and the months and the revolutions of the years have created number and have given us a conception of time, and the power of inquiring about the nature of the universe; and from this source we have derived philosophy, than which no greater good ever was or will be given by the gods to mortal man. This is the greatest boon of sight; and of the lesser benefits why should I speak? Even the ordinary man if he were deprived of them would bewail his loss, but in vain. Thus much let me say however: God invented and gave us sight to the end that we might behold the courses of intelligence in the heaven, and apply them to the courses of our own intelligence which are akin to them, the unperturbed to the perturbed; and that we, learning them and partaking of the natural truth of reason, might imitate the absolutely unerring courses of God and regulate our own vagaries. The same may be affirmed of speech and hearing: they have been given by the gods to the same end and for a like reason. For this is the principal end of speech, whereto it most contributes. Moreover, so much of music as is adapted to the sound of the voice[21] and to the sense of hearing is granted to us for the sake of harmony; and harmony, which has motions akin to the revolutions of our souls, is not regarded by the intelligent votary of the Muses as given by them with a view to irrational pleasure, which is deemed to be the purpose of it in our day, but as meant to correct any discord which may have arisen in the courses of the soul, and to be our ally in bringing her into harmony and agreement with herself; and rhythm too was given by them for the same reason, on account of the irregular and graceless ways which prevail among mankind generally, and to help us against them.

Thus far in what we have been saying, with small exceptions, the works of intelligence have been set forth; and now we must place by the side of them in our discourse the things which come into being through necessity—for the creation is mixed, being made up of necessity and mind. Mind, the ruling power, persuaded necessity to bring the greater part of created things to perfection, and thus and after this manner in the beginning, when the influence of reason got the better of necessity, the universe was created. But if a person will truly tell of the way in which the work was accomplished, he must include the other influence of the variable cause as well. Wherefore, we must return again and find another suitable beginning, as about the former matters, so also about these. To which end we must consider the nature of fire and water and air and earth, such as they were prior to the creation of the heaven, and what was happening to them in this previous state;[22] for no one has as yet explained the manner of their generation, but we speak of fire and the rest of them, whatever they mean, as though men knew their natures, and we maintain them to be the first principles and letters or elements of the whole, when they cannot reasonably be compared by· a man of any sense even to syllables or first compounds. And let me say thus much: I will not now speak of the first principle or principles of all things, or by whatever name they are to be called, for this reason—because it is difficult to set forth my

48

[21] Reading φωνῇ and placing the comma after ἀκοήν.

[22] Cp. *infra*, 53a.

opinion according to the method of discussion which we are at present employing. Do not imagine, any more than I can bring myself to imagine, that I should be right in undertaking so great and difficult a task. Remembering what I said at first about probability, I will do my best to give as probable an explanation as any other— or rather, more probable; and I will first go back to the beginning and try to speak of each thing and of all.[23] Once more, then, at the commencement of my discourse, I call upon God and beg him to be our savior out of a strange and unwonted inquiry, and to bring us to the haven of probability. So now let us begin again.

This new beginning of our discussion of the universe requires a fuller division than the former; for then we made two classes, now a third must be revealed. The two sufficed for the former discussion: one, which we assumed, was a pattern intelligible and always the same; and the second was only the imitation of the pattern, generated and visible. There is also a third kind which we did not distinguish at the time, conceiving that the two would be enough. But now the argument seems to require that we should set forth in words another kind, which is difficult of explanation and dimly seen. What nature are we to attribute to this new kind of being? We reply that it is the receptacle, and in a manner the nurse, of all generation. I have spoken the truth, but I must express myself in clearer language, and this will be an arduous task for many reasons, and in particular because I must first raise questions concerning fire and the other elements, and determine what each of them is; for to say, with any probability or certitude, which of them should be called water rather than fire, and which should be called any of them rather than all or some one of them, is a difficult matter. How, then, shall we settle this point, and what questions about the elements may be fairly raised?

In the first place, we see that what we just now called water, by condensation, I suppose, becomes stone and earth; and this same element, when melted and dispersed, passes into vapor and air. Air, again, when inflamed, becomes fire; and, again, fire, when condensed and extinguished, passes once more into the form of air; and

49

[23] Putting the comma after μᾶλλον δέ; or, following Stallbaum and omitting the comma, "or rather, before entering on this probable discussion, we will begin again, and try to speak of each thing and of all."

once more, air, when collected and condensed, produces cloud and mist; and from these, when still more compressed, comes flowing water, and from water comes earth and stones once more; and thus generation appears to be transmitted from one to the other in a circle. Thus, then, as the several elements never present themselves in the same form, how can any one have the assurance to assert positively that any of them, whatever it may be, is one thing rather than another? No one can. But much the safest plan is to speak of them as follows: Anything which we see to be continually changing, as, for example, fire, we must not call "this" or "that," but rather say that it is "of such a nature"; nor let us speak of water as "this," but always as "such"; nor must we imply that there is any stability in any of those things which we indicate by the use of the words "this" and "that," supposing ourselves to signify something thereby; for they are too volatile to be detained in any such expressions as "this," or "that," or "relative to this," or any other mode of speaking which represents them as permanent. We ought not to apply "this" to any of them, but rather the word "such," which expresses the similar principle circulating in each and all of them; for example, that should be called "fire" which is of such a nature always, and so of everything that has generation. That in which the elements severally grow up, and appear, and decay, is alone to be called by the name "this" or "that"; but that

50   which is of a certain nature, hot or white, or anything which admits of opposite qualities, and all things that are compounded of them, ought not to be so denominated. Let me make another attempt to explain my meaning more clearly. Suppose a person to make all kinds of figures of gold and to be always transmuting one form into all the rest; somebody points to one of them and asks what it is. By far the safest and truest answer is, That is gold; and not to call the triangle or any other figures which are formed in the gold "these," as though they had existence, since they are in process of change while he is making the assertion; but if the questioner be willing to take the safe and indefinite expression, "such," we should be satisfied. And the same argument applies to the universal nature which receives all bodies—that must be always called the same; for, while receiving all things, she never departs at all from her own nature and never, in any way or at any time, assumes a

form like that of any of the things which enter into her; she is the natural recipient of all impressions, and is stirred and informed by them, and appears different from time to time by reason of them. But the forms which enter into and go out of her are the likenesses of real existences modeled after their patterns in a wonderful and inexplicable manner, which we will hereafter investigate. For the present we have only to conceive of three natures: first, that which is in process of generation; secondly, that in which the generation takes place; and thirdly, that of which the thing generated is a resemblance. And we may liken the receiving principle to a mother, and the source or spring to a father, and the intermediate nature to a child; and may remark further that if the model is to take every variety of form, then the matter in which the model is fashioned will not be duly prepared unless it is formless and free from the impress of any of those shapes which it is hereafter to receive from without. For if the matter were like any of the supervening forms, then whenever any opposite or entirely different nature was stamped upon its surface, it would take the impression badly, because it would intrude its own shape. Wherefore that which is to receive all forms should have no form; as in making perfumes they first contrive that the liquid substance which is to receive the scent shall be as inodorous as possible; or as those who wish to impress figures on soft substances do not allow any previous impression to remain, but begin by making the surface as even and smooth as possible. In the same way that which is to receive perpetually and through its whole extent the resemblances of all eternal beings ought to be devoid of any particular form. Wherefore the mother and receptacle of all created and visible and in any way sensible things is not to be termed earth or air or fire or water, or any of their compounds, or any of the elements from which these are derived, but is an invisible and formless being which receives all things and in some mysterious way partakes of the intelligible, and is most incomprehensible. In saying this we shall not be far wrong; as far, however, as we can attain to a knowledge of her from the previous considerations, we may truly say that fire is that part of her nature which from time to time is inflamed, and water that which is moistened, and that the mother substance becomes earth and air, in so far as she receives the impressions of them.

51

33

Let us consider this question more precisely. Is there any self-existent fire, and do all those things which we call "self-existent" exist, or are only those things which we see or in some way perceive through the bodily organs truly existent, and nothing whatever besides them? And is all that which we call an intelligible essence nothing at all, and only a name? Here is a question which we must not leave unexplained or undetermined, nor must we affirm too confidently that there can be no decision;[24] neither must we interpolate in our present long discourse a digression equally long; but if it is possible to set forth a great principle in a few words, that is just what we want.

Thus I state my view: If mind and true opinion are two distinct classes, then I say that there certainly are these self-existent ideas unperceived by sense, and apprehended only by the mind; if, however, as some say, true opinion differs in no respect from mind, then everything that we perceive through the body is to be regarded as most real and certain. But we must affirm them to be distinct, for they have a distinct origin and are of a different nature; the one is implanted in us by instruction, the other by persuasion; the one is always accompanied by true reason, the other is without reason; the one cannot be overcome by persuasion, but the other can; and lastly, every man may be said to share in true opinion, but mind is the attribute of the gods and of very few men. Wherefore also we must acknowledge that there is one kind of being which is always the same, uncreated and indestructible, never receiving anything into itself from without, nor itself going out to any other, but invisible and imperceptible by any sense, and of which the contemplation is granted to intelligence only. And there is another nature of the same name with it, and like to it, perceived by sense, created, always in motion, becoming in place and again vanishing out of place, which is apprehended by opinion and sense. And there is a third nature, which is space and is eternal, and admits not of de-

[24] [Jowett has clearly misunderstood Plato's text. The question at issue concerns Plato's fundamental doctrine, that there are "intelligible essences"— that is, Ideas—over and above the sense-objects we perceive. This is a question, Plato says, that we cannot leave unsettled, nor should we merely affirm dogmatically that there are such essences. He proceeds to give a brief argument for the doctrine, in lieu of the more extensive justification that it would be possible to give, but which would be out of place here.—*Ed.*]

struction and provides a home for all created things, and is apprehended without the help of sense, by a kind of spurious reason, and is hardly real; which we beholding as in a dream, say of all existence that it must of necessity be in some place and occupy a space, but that what is neither in heaven nor in earth has no existence. Of these and other things of the same kind, relating to the true and waking reality of nature, we have only this dream-like sense, and we are unable to cast off sleep and determine the truth about them. For an image, since the reality after which it is modeled does not belong to it,[25] and it exists ever as the fleeting shadow of some other, must be inferred to be in another [that is, in space], grasping existence in some way or other, or it could not be at all. But true and exact reason, vindicating the nature of true being, maintains that while two things [that is, the image and space] are different they cannot exist one of them in the other and so be one and also two at the same time.

Thus have I concisely given the result of my thoughts; and my verdict is that being and space and generation, these three, existed in their three ways before the heaven; and that the nurse of generation, moistened by water and inflamed by fire, and receiving the forms of earth and air, and experiencing all the affections which accompany these, presented a strange variety of appearances; and being full of powers which were neither similar nor equally balanced, was never in any part in a state of equipoise, but swaying unevenly hither and thither, was shaken by them, and by its motion again shook them; and the elements when moved were separated and carried continually, some one way, some another; as, when grain is shaken and winnowed by fans and other instruments used in the threshing of corn, the close and heavy particles are borne away and settle in one direction, and the loose and light particles in another. In this manner, the four kinds or elements were then shaken by the receiving vessel, which, moving like a winnowing machine, scattered far away from one another the elements most unlike, and forced the most similar elements into close contact. Wherefore also the various elements had different places before they were arranged so as to form the universe. At first, they

53

<hr/>

[25] Or, "since in its very intention it is not self-existent"—which, though obscure, avoids any inaccuracy of construction.

were all without reason and measure. But when the world began to get into order, fire and water and earth and air had only certain faint traces of themselves, and were altogether such as everything might be expected to be in the absence of God; this, I say, was their nature at that time, and God fashioned them by form and number. Let it be consistently maintained by us in all that we say that God made them as far as possible the fairest and best, out of things which were not fair and good. And now I will endeavor to show you the disposition and generation of them by an unaccustomed argument which I am compelled to use; but I believe that you will be able to follow me, for your education has made you familiar with the methods of science.[26]

In the first place, then, as is evident to all, fire and earth and water and air are bodies. And every sort of body possesses solidity, and every solid must necessarily be contained in planes; and every plane rectilinear figure is composed of triangles; and all triangles are originally of two kinds, both of which are made up of one right and two acute angles; one of them has at either end of the base the half of a divided right angle, having equal sides, while in the other the right angle is divided into unequal parts, having unequal sides. These, then, proceeding by a combination of probability with demonstration, we assume to be the original elements of fire and the other bodies; but the principles which are prior to these God only knows, and he of men who is the friend of God. And next we have to determine what are the four most beautiful bodies which are unlike one another, and of which some are capable of resolution into one another; for having discovered thus much, we shall know the true origin of earth and fire and of the proportionate and intermediate elements. And then we shall not be willing to allow that there are any distinct kinds of visible bodies fairer than these. Wherefore we must endeavor to construct the four forms of bodies which excel in beauty, and then we shall be able to say that we have sufficiently apprehended their nature. Now of the two triangles, the isosceles has one form only; the scalene or unequal-sided has an infinite number. Of the infinite forms we must select the most beautiful, if we are to proceed in due order, and any one who can point

54

[26] [Better, "familiar with those methods (or branches of learning) which this exposition requires."—*Ed.*]

out a more beautiful form than ours for the construction of these bodies, shall carry off the palm, not as an enemy, but as a friend. Now, the one which we maintain to be the most beautiful of all the many triangles (and we need not speak of the others) is that of which the double forms a third triangle which is equilateral; the reason of this would be long to tell; he who disproves what we are saying, and shows that we are mistaken, may claim a friendly victory. Then let us choose two triangles, out of which fire and the other elements have been constructed, one isosceles, the other having the square of the longer side equal to three times the square of the lesser side.

Now is the time to explain what was before obscurely said: there was an error in imagining that all the four elements might be generated by and into one another; this, I say, was an erroneous supposition, for there are generated from the triangles which we have selected four kinds—three from the one which has the sides unequal; the fourth alone is framed out of the isosceles triangle. Hence they cannot all be resolved into one another, a great number of small bodies being combined into a few large ones, or the converse. But three of them can be thus resolved and compounded, for they all spring from one, and when the greater bodies are broken up, many small bodies will spring up out of them and take their own proper figures; or, again, when many small bodies are dissolved into their triangles, if they become one, they will form one large mass of another kind. So much for their passage into one another. I have now to speak of their several kinds, and show out of what combinations of numbers each of them was formed. The first will be the simplest and smallest construction, and its element is that triangle which has its hypotenuse twice the lesser side. When two such triangles are joined at the diagonal, and this is repeated three times, and the triangles rest their diagonals and shorter sides on the same point as a center, a single equilateral triangle is formed out of six triangles; and four equilateral triangles, if put together, make out of every three plane angles one solid angle, being that which is nearest to the most obtuse of plane angles; and out of the combination of these four angles arises the first solid form which distributes into equal and similar parts the whole circle in which it is inscribed. The second species of solid is formed out of

55

37

the same triangles, which unite as eight equilateral triangles and form one solid angle out of four plane angles, and out of six such angles the second body is completed. And the third body is made up of 120 triangular elements, forming twelve solid angles, each of them included in five plane equilateral triangles, having altogether twenty bases, each of which is an equilateral triangle. The one element [that is, the triangle which has its hypotenuse twice the lesser side], having generated these figures, generated no more; but the isosceles triangle produced the fourth elementary figure, which is compounded of four such triangles, joining their right angles in a center, and forming one equilateral quadrangle. Six of these united form eight solid angles, each of which is made by the combination of three plane right angles; the figure of the body thus composed is a cube, having six plane quadrangular equilateral bases. There was yet a fifth combination which God used in the delineation of the universe.

Now he who, duly reflecting on all this, inquires whether the worlds are to be regarded as indefinite or definite in number, will be of opinion that the notion of their indefiniteness is characteristic of a sadly indefinite and ignorant mind. He, however, who raises the question whether they are to be truly regarded as one or five, takes up a more reasonable position. Arguing from probabilities, I am of opinion that they are one; another, regarding the question from another point of view, will be of another mind. But, leaving this inquiry, let us proceed to distribute the elementary forms, which have now been created in idea, among the four elements.

To earth, then, let us assign the cubical form; for earth is the most immovable of the four and the most plastic of all bodies, and that which has the most stable bases must of necessity be of such a nature. Now, of the triangles which we assumed at first, that which has two equal sides is by nature more firmly based than that which has unequal sides; and of the compound figures which are formed out of either, the plane equilateral quadrangle has necessarily a more stable basis than the equilateral triangle, both in the whole and in the parts. Wherefore, in assigning this figure to earth, we adhere to probability; and to water we assign that one of the remaining forms which is the least movable; and the most movable of them, to fire; and to air that which is intermediate.

56

Also we assign the smallest body to fire, and the greatest to water, and the intermediate in size to air; and, again, the acutest body to fire, and the next in acuteness to air, and the third to water. Of all these elements, that which has the fewest bases must necessarily be the most movable, for it must be the acutest and most penetrating in every way, and also the lightest as being composed of the smallest number of similar particles; and the second body has similar properties in a second degree, and the third body, in the third degree. Let it be agreed, then, both according to strict reason and according to probability, that the pyramid is the solid which is the original element and seed of fire; and let us assign the element which was next in the order of generation to air, and the third to water. We must imagine all these to be so small that no single particle of any of the four kinds is seen by us on account of their smallness; but when many of them are collected together, their aggregates are seen. And the ratios of their numbers, motions, and other properties, everywhere God, as far as necessity allowed or gave consent, has exactly perfected and harmonized in due proportion.

From all that we have just been saying about the elements or kinds, the most probable conclusion is as follows: earth, when meeting with fire and dissolved by its sharpness, whether the dissolution take place in the fire itself or perhaps in some mass of air or water, is borne hither and thither until its parts, meeting together and mutually harmonizing, again become earth; for they can never take any other form. But water, when divided by fire or by air, on re-forming, may become one part fire and two parts air; and a single volume of air divided becomes two of fire. Again, when a small body of fire is contained in a larger body of air or water or earth, and both are moving, and the fire struggling is overcome and broken up, then two volumes of fire form one volume of air; and when air is overcome and cut up into small pieces, two and a half parts of air are condensed into one part of water. Let us consider the matter in another way: when one of the other elements is fastened upon by fire and is cut by the sharpness of its angles and sides, it coalesces with the fire, and then ceases to be cut by them any longer. For no element which is one and the same with itself can be changed by or change another of the same kind and in the same state. But so long as in the process of transition the weaker is fighting against the stronger, the dissolution continues. Again, when a few small particles, enclosed in many larger ones, are in process of decomposition and extinction, they only cease from their tendency to extinction when they consent to pass into the conquering nature, and fire becomes air and air water. But if bodies of another kind go and attack them [that is, the small particles], the latter continue to be dissolved until, being completely forced back and dispersed, they make their escape to their own kindred, or else, being overcome and assimilated to the conquering power, they remain where they are and dwell with their victors, and from being many become one. And owing to these affections, all things are changing their place, for by the motion of the receiving vessel the bulk of each class is distributed into its proper place; but those things which become unlike themselves and like other things are hurried by the shaking into the place of the things to which they grow like.

Now all unmixed and primary bodies are produced by such causes as these. As to the subordinate species which are included in the greater kinds, they are to be attributed to the varieties in the structure of the two original triangles. For either structure did not originally produce the triangle of one size only, but some larger and some smaller, and there are as many sizes as there are species of the four elements. Hence when they are mingled with themselves and with one another there is an endless variety of them, which those who would arrive at the probable truth of nature ought duly to consider.

Unless a person comes to an understanding about the nature and conditions of rest and motion, he will meet with many difficulties in the discussion which follows. Something has been said of this matter already, and something more remains to be said—which is that motion never exists in what is uniform. For to conceive that anything can be moved without a mover is hard or indeed impossible, and equally impossible to conceive that there can be a mover unless there be something which can be moved—motion cannot exist where either of these are wanting, and for these to be uniform is impossible; wherefore we must assign rest to uniformity and motion to the want of uniformity. Now inequality is the cause of the nature which is wanting in uniformity; and of this we have al-

58

eady described the origin. But there still remains the further point —why things when divided after their kinds do not cease to pass through one another and to change their place—which we will now proceed to explain. In the revolution of the universe are comprehended all the four elements, and this being circular and having a tendency to come together, compresses everything and will not allow any place to be left void. Wherefore also fire, above all things, penetrates everywhere, and air next, as being next in rarity of the elements; and the two other elements in like manner penetrate according to their degrees of rarity. For those things which are composed of the largest particles have the largest void left in their compositions, and those which are composed of the smallest particles have the least. And the contraction caused by the compression thrusts the smaller particles into the interstices of the larger. And thus, when the small parts are placed side by side with the larger, and the lesser divide the greater and the greater unite the lesser, all the elements are borne up and down and hither and thither toward their own places; for the change in the size of each changes its position in space. And these causes generate an inequality which is always maintained, and is continually creating a perpetual motion of the elements in all time.

In the next place we have to consider that there are divers kinds of fire. There are, for example, first, flame; and secondly, those emanations of flame which do not burn but only give light to the eyes; thirdly, the remains of fire, which are seen in red-hot embers after the flame has been extinguished. There are similar differences in the air; of which the brightest part is called the aether, and the most turbid sort mist and darkness; and there are various other nameless kinds which arise from the inequality of the triangles. Water, again, admits in the first place of a division into two kinds: the one liquid and the other fusile. The liquid kind is composed of the small and unequal particles of water, and moves itself and is moved by other bodies owing to the want of uniformity and the shape of its particles; whereas the fusile kind, being formed of large and uniform particles, is more stable than the other and is heavy and compact by reason of its uniformity. But when fire gets in and dissolves the particles and destroys the uniformity, it has greater mobility, and becoming fluid is thrust forth by the neighboring air and spreads upon the earth; and this dissolution of the solid masses is called melting, and their spreading out upon the earth flowing. Again, when the fire goes out of the fusile substance, it does not pass into a vacuum, but into the neighboring air; and the air which is displaced forces together the liquid and still moveable mass into the place which was occupied by the fire, and unites it with itself. Thus compressed the mass resumes its equability, and is again at unity with itself, because the fire which was the author of the inequality has retreated; and this departure of the fire is called cooling, and the coming together which follows upon it is termed congealment. Of all the kinds termed fusile, that which is the densest and is formed out of the finest and most uniform parts is that most precious possession called gold, which is hardened by filtration through rock; this is unique in kind, and has both a glittering and a yellow color. A shoot of gold, which is so dense as to be very hard, and takes a black color, is termed adamant. There is also another kind which has parts nearly like gold, and of which there are several species; it is denser than gold, and it contains a small and fine portion of earth and is therefore harder, yet also lighter because of the great interstices which it has within itself; and this substance which is one of the bright and denser kinds of water, when solidified is called copper. There is an alloy of earth mingled with it which, when the two parts grow old and are disunited, shows itself separately and is called rust. The remaining phenomena of the same kind there will be no difficulty in reasoning out by the method of probabilities. A man may sometimes set aside meditations about eternal things, and for recreation turn to consider the truths of generation, which are probable only; he will thus gain a pleasure not to be repented of, and secure for himself, while he lives, a wise and moderate pastime. Let us grant ourselves this indulgence and go through the probabilities relating to the same subjects which follow next in order.

Water which is mingled with fire, so much as is fine and liquid (being so called by reason of its motion and the way in which it rolls along the ground), and soft, because its bases give way and are less stable than those of earth, when separated from fire and air and isolated, becomes more uniform, and by their retirement is compressed into itself; and if the condensation be very great, the water above the earth becomes hail, but on the earth, ice; and that which is congealed in a less degree and is only half solid, when above the earth is called snow, and when upon the earth and condensed from dew, hoarfrost. Then, again, there are the numerous kinds of water which have been mingled with one another and are distilled through plants which grow in the earth; and this whole class is called by the name of juices or saps. The unequal admixture of these fluids creates a variety of species—most of them are nameless, but four which are of a fiery nature are clearly distinguished and have names. First, there is wine, which warms the soul as well as the body; secondly, there is the oily nature, which is smooth and divides the visual ray, and for this reason is bright and shining and of a glistening appearance, including pitch, the juice of the castor berry, oil itself, and other things of a like kind; thirdly, there is the class of substances which expand the contracted parts[27] of the mouth, until they return to their natural state, and by reason of this property create sweetness—these are included under the general name of honey; and, lastly, there is a frothy nature which differs from all juices, having a burning quality which dissolves the flesh; it is called *opos* (a vegetable acid).

As to the kinds of earth, that which is filtered through water passes into stone in the following manner: The water which mixes with the earth and is broken up in the process changes into air, and taking this form mounts into its own place. But as there is no surrounding vacuum it thrusts away the neighboring air, and this being rendered heavy, and, when it is displaced, having been poured around the mass of earth, forcibly compresses it and drives it into the vacant space whence the new air had come up; and the earth when compressed by the air into an indissoluble union with water becomes rock. The fairer sort is that which is made up of equal and similar parts and is transparent; that which has the opposite qualities is inferior. But when all the watery part is suddenly drawn out by fire, a more brittle substance is formed to which we give the name of pottery. Sometimes also moisture may remain, and the earth which has been fused by fire becomes, when cool, a certain stone of a black color. A like separation of the water which had been copiously mingled with them may occur in two substances

[27] Cp. 65c, 66c.

composed of finer particles of earth and of a briny nature; out of either of them a half-solid body is then formed, soluble in water— the one, soda, which is used for purging away oil and earth, the other, salt, which harmonizes so well in combinations pleasing to the palate, and is, as the law testifies, a substance dear to the gods. The compounds of earth and water are not soluble by water, but by fire only, and for this reason: neither fire nor air melt masses of earth; for their particles, being smaller than the interstices in its structure, have plenty of room to move without forcing their way, and so they leave the earth unmelted and undissolved; but particles of water, which are larger, force a passage and dissolve and melt the earth. Wherefore earth when not consolidated by force is dissolved by water only; when consolidated, by nothing but fire; for this is the only body which can find an entrance. The cohesion of water again, when very strong, is dissolved by fire only; when weaker, then either by air or fire—the former entering the interstices, and the latter penetrating even the triangles. But nothing can dissolve air, when strongly condensed, which does not reach the elements or triangles; or if not strongly condensed, then only fire can dissolve it. As to bodies composed of earth and water, while the water occupies the vacant interstices of the earth in them which are compressed by force, the particles of water which approach them from without, finding no entrance, flow around the entire mass and leave it undissolved; but the particles of fire, entering into the interstices of the water, do to the water what water does to earth and fire to air,[28] and are the sole causes of the compound body of earth and water liquefying and becoming fluid. Now these bodies are of two kinds; some of them, such as glass and the fusible sort of stones, have less water than they have earth; on the other hand, substances of the nature of wax and incense have more of water entering into their composition.

I have thus shown the various classes of bodies as they are diversified by their forms and combinations and changes into one another, and now I must endeavor to set forth their affections and the causes of them. In the first place, the bodies which I have been describing are necessarily objects of sense. But we have not yet considered the origin of flesh, or what belongs to flesh, or of that

[28] The text seems to be corrupt.

part of the soul which is mortal. And these things cannot be adequately explained without also explaining the affections which are concerned with sensation, nor the latter without the former; and yet to explain them together is hardly possible; for which reason we must assume first one or the other and afterwards examine the nature of our hypothesis.[29] In order, then, that the affections may follow regularly after the elements, let us presuppose the existence of body and soul.

First, let us inquire what we mean by saying that fire is hot; and about this we may reason from the dividing or cutting power which it exercises on our bodies. We all of us feel that fire is sharp; and we may further consider the fineness of the sides, and the sharpness of the angles, and the smallness of the particles, and the swiftness of the motion—all this makes the action of fire violent and sharp, so that it cuts whatever it meets. And we must not forget that the original figure of fire [that is, the pyramid], more than any other form, has a dividing power which cuts our bodies into small pieces (κερματίζει), and thus naturally produces that affection which we call heat; and hence the origin of the name (θερμὸς, κέρμα). Now, the opposite of this is sufficiently manifest; nevertheless we will not fail to describe it. For the larger particles of moisture which surround the body, entering in and driving out the lesser, but not being able to take their places, compress the moist principle in us; and this, from being unequal and disturbed, is forced by them into a state of rest which is due to equability and compression. But things which are contracted contrary to nature are by nature at war and force themselves apart; and to this war and convulsion the name of shivering and trembling is given; and the whole affection and the cause of the affection are both termed cold. That is called hard to which our flesh yields, and soft which yields to our flesh; and things are also termed hard and soft relatively to one another. That which yields has a small base; but that which rests on quadrangular bases is firmly posed and belongs to the class which offers the greatest resistance; so, too, does that which is the most compact and therefore most repellent. The nature of the light and the heavy will be best understood when examined in connection with our notions of above and below; for it

[29] Omitting ὕστερα.

is quite a mistake to suppose that the universe is parted into two regions, separate from and opposite to each other—the one a lower to which all things tend which have any bulk, and an upper to which things only ascend against their will. For as the universe is in the form of a sphere, all the extremities, being equidistant from the center, are equally extremities, and the center, which is equidistant from them, is equally to be regarded as the opposite of them all. Such being the nature of the world, when a person says that any of these points is above or below, may he not be justly charged with using an improper expression? For the center of the world cannot be rightly called either above or below, but is the center and nothing else; and the circumference is not the center, and has in no one part of itself a different relation to the center from what it has in any of the opposite parts. Indeed, when it is in every direction similar, how can one rightly give to it names which imply opposition? For if there were any solid body in equipoise at the center of the universe, there would be nothing to draw it to this extreme rather than to that, for they are all perfectly similar; and if a person were to go round the world in a circle, he would often, when standing at the antipodes of his former position, speak of the same point as above and below; for, as I was saying just now, to speak of the whole which is in the form of a globe as having one part above and another below is not like a sensible man. The reason why these names are used, and the circumstances under which they are ordinarily applied by us to the division of the heavens, may be elucidated by the following supposition: If a person were to stand in that part of the universe which is the appointed place of fire, and where there is the great mass of fire to which fiery bodies gather— if, I say, he were to ascend thither, and, having the power to do this, were to abstract particles of fire and put them in scales and weigh them, and then, raising the balance, were to draw the fire by force toward the uncongenial element of the air, it would be very evident that he could compel the smaller mass more readily than the larger; for when two things are simultaneously raised by one and the same power, the smaller body must necessarily yield to the superior power with less reluctance than the larger; and the larger body is called heavy and said to tend downward, and the smaller body is called light and said to tend upward. And we may detect

63

ourselves who are upon the earth doing precisely the same thing. For we often separate earthy natures, and sometimes earth itself, and draw them into the uncongenial element of air by force and contrary to nature, both clinging to their kindred elements. But that which is smaller yields to the impulse given by us toward the dissimilar element more easily than the larger; and so we call the former light, and the place toward which it is impelled we call above, and the contrary state and place we call heavy and below respectively. Now the relations of these must necessarily vary because the principal masses of the different elements hold opposite positions; for that which is light, heavy, below or above in one place will be found to be and become contrary and transverse and every way diverse in relation to that which is light, heavy, below or above in an opposite place. And about all of them this has to be considered—that the tendency of each toward its kindred element makes the body which is moved heavy, and the place toward which the motion tends below, but things which have an opposite tendency we call by an opposite name. Such are the causes which we assign to these phenomena. As to the smooth and the rough, any one who sees them can explain the reason of them to another. For roughness is hardness mingled with irregularity, and smoothness is produced by the joint effect of uniformity and density.

The most important of the affections which concern the whole body remains to be considered—that is, the cause of pleasure and pain in the perceptions of which I have been speaking, and in all other things which are perceived by sense through the parts of the body, and have both pains and pleasures attendant on them. Let us imagine the causes of every affection, whether of sense or not, to be of the following nature, remembering that we have already distinguished between the nature which is easy and which is hard to move; for this is the direction in which we must hunt the prey which we mean to take. A body which is of a nature to be easily moved, on receiving an impression however slight, spreads abroad the motion in a circle, the parts communicating with each other, until at last, reaching the principle of mind, they announce the quality of the agent. But a body of the opposite kind, being immobile and not extending to the surrounding region, merely receives the impression and does not stir any of the neighboring parts; and since the parts do not distribute the original impression to other parts, it has no effect of motion on the whole animal, and therefore produces no effect on the patient. This is true of the bones and hair and other more earthy parts of the human body; whereas what was said above relates mainly to sight and hearing because they have in them the greatest amount of fire and air. Now we must conceive of pleasure and pain in this way: an impression produced in us contrary to nature and violent, if sudden, is painful; and, again, the sudden return to nature is pleasant; but a gentle and gradual return is imperceptible and *vice versa*. On the other hand, the impression of sense which is most easily produced is most readily felt, but is not accompanied by pleasure or pain; such, for example, are the affections of the sight, which, as we said above, is a body naturally uniting with our body in the daytime (45); for cuttings and burnings and other affections which happen to the sight do not give pain, nor is there pleasure when the sight returns to its natural state; but the sensations are clearest and strongest according to the manner in which the eye is affected by the object, and itself strikes and touches it; there is no violence either in the contraction or dilation of the eye. But bodies formed of larger particles yield to the agent only with a struggle; and then they impart their motions to the whole and cause pleasure and pain—pain when alienated from their natural conditions, and pleasure when restored to them. Things which experience gradual withdrawings and emptyings of their nature, and great and sudden replenishments, fail to perceive the emptying, but are sensible of the replenishment; and so they occasion no pain, but the greatest pleasure, to the mortal part of the soul, as is manifest in the case of perfumes. But things which are changed all of a sudden, and only gradually and with difficulty return to their own nature, have effects in every way opposite to the former, as is evident in the case of burnings and cuttings of the body.

Thus have we discussed the general affections of the whole body, and the names of the agents which produce them. And now I will endeavor to speak of the affections of particular parts, and the causes and agents of them, as far as I am able. In the first place, let us set forth what was omitted when we were speaking of juices, concerning the affections peculiar to the tongue. These too, like most of the other affections, appear to be caused by certain contractions and dilations, but they have besides more of roughness and smoothness than is found in other affections; for whenever earthy particles enter into the small veins which are the testing instruments of the tongue, reaching to the heart, and fall upon the moist, delicate portions of flesh—when, as they are dissolved, they contract and dry up the little veins, they are astringent if they are rougher, but if not so rough, then only harsh. Those of them which are of an abstergent nature and purge the whole surface of the tongue, if they do it in excess and so encroach as to consume some part of the flesh itself, like potash and soda, are all termed bitter. But the particles which are deficient in the alkaline quality, and which cleanse only moderately, are called salt, and having no bitterness or roughness are regarded as rather agreeable than otherwise. Bodies which share in and are made smooth by the heat of the mouth, and which are inflamed and again in turn inflame that which heats them, and which are so light that they are carried upward to the sensations of the head and cut all that comes in their way, by reason of these qualities in them, are all termed pungent. 66

But when these same particles, refined by putrefaction, enter into the narrow veins and are duly proportioned to the particles of earth and air which are there, they set them whirling about one another, and while they are in a whirl cause them to dash against and enter into one another, and so form hollows surrounding the particles that enter—which watery vessels of air (for a film of moisture, sometimes earthy, sometimes pure, is spread around the air) are hollow spheres of water; and those of them which are pure are transparent and are called bubbles, while those composed of the earthy liquid, which is in a state of general agitation and effervescence, are said to boil or ferment—of all these affections the cause is termed acid. And there is the opposite affection arising from an opposite cause, when the mass of entering particles, immersed in the moisture of the mouth, is congenial to the tongue, and smooths and oils over the roughness, and relaxes the parts which are unnaturally contracted, and contracts the parts which are relaxed, and disposes them all according to their nature—that sort of remedy of violent affections is pleasant and agreeable to every man, and has the name sweet. But enough of this.

The faculty of smell does not admit of differences of kind; for all smells are of a half-formed nature, and no element is so proportioned as to have any smell. The veins about the nose are too narrow to admit earth and water, and too wide to detain fire and air; and for this reason no one ever perceives the smell of any of them; but smells always proceed from bodies that are damp, or putrefying, or liquefying, or evaporating, and are perceptible only in the intermediate state, when water is changing into air and air into water; and all of them are either vapor or mist. That which is passing out of air into water is mist, and that which is passing from water into air is vapor; and hence all smells are thinner than water and thicker than air. The proof of this is that when there is any obstruction to the respiration and a man draws in his breath by force, then no smell filters through, but the air without the smell alone penetrates. Wherefore the varieties of smell have no name, and they have not many or definite and simple kinds; but they are distinguished only as painful and pleasant, the one sort irritating and disturbing the whole cavity which is situated between the head and the navel, the other having a soothing influence and restoring this same region to an agreeable and natural condition.

In considering the third kind of sense, hearing, we must speak of the causes in which it originates. We may in general assume sound to be a blow which passes through the ears, and is transmitted by means of the air, the brain, and the blood, to the soul, and that hearing is the vibration of this blow which begins in the head and ends in the region of the liver. The sound which moves swiftly is acute, and the sound which moves slowly is grave, and that which is regular is equable and smooth, and the reverse is harsh. A great body of sound is loud, and a small body of sound the reverse. Respecting the harmonies of sound I must hereafter speak.

There is a fourth class of sensible things, having many intricate varieties, which must now be distinguished. They are called by the general name of colors and are a flame which emanates from every sort of body, and has particles corresponding to the sense of sight. I have spoken already, in what has preceded, of the causes which generate sight, and in this place it will be natural and suitable to give a rational theory of colors.

Of the particles coming from other bodies which fall upon the sight, some are smaller and some are larger, and some are equal to the parts of the sight itself. Those which are equal are imperceptible, and we call them transparent. The larger produce contraction, the smaller dilation, in the sight, exercising a power akin to that of hot and cold bodies on the flesh, or of astringent bodies on the tongue, or of those heating bodies which we termed pungent. White and black are similar effects of contraction and dilation in another sphere, and for this reason have a different appearance. Wherefore we ought to term white that which dilates the visual ray, and the opposite of this is black. There is also a swifter motion of a different sort of fire which strikes and dilates the ray of sight until it reaches the eyes, forcing a way through their passages and melting them, and eliciting from them a union of fire and water which we call tears, being itself an opposite fire which comes to them from an opposite direction—the inner fire flashes forth like lightning, and the outer finds a way in and is extinguished in the moisture, and all sorts of colors are generated by the mixture. This affection is termed dazzling, and the object which produces it is called bright and flashing. There is another sort of fire which is intermediate and which reaches and mingles with the moisture of the eye without flashing; and in this the fire, mingling with the ray of the moisture, produces a color like blood, to which we give the name of red. A bright hue mingled with red and white gives the color called auburn ($\xi\alpha\nu\theta\acute{o}\nu$). The law of proportion, however, according to which the several colors are formed, even if a man knew he would be foolish in telling, for he could not give any necessary reason, nor indeed any tolerable or probable explanation of them. Again, red, when mingled with black and white, becomes purple, but it becomes umber ($\acute{o}\rho\varphi\nu\iota\nu\nu$) when the colors are burnt as well as mingled and the black is more thoroughly mixed with them. Flame color ($\pi\nu\rho\rho\grave{o}\nu$) is produced by a union of auburn and dun ($\varphi\alpha\iota\grave{o}\nu$), and dun by an admixture of black and white; pale yellow ($\grave{\omega}\chi\rho\grave{o}\nu$), by an admixture of white and auburn. White and bright meeting, and falling upon a full black, become dark blue ($\kappa\nu\alpha\nu\sigma\hat{\nu}\nu$), and when dark blue mingles with white, a light blue ($\gamma\lambda\alpha\nu\kappa\grave{o}\nu$) color is formed, as flame color with black makes leek green ($\pi\rho\acute{\alpha}\sigma\iota\sigma\nu$). There will be no difficulty in seeing how and by what mixtures the colors derived from these are made according to the rules of probability. He, however, who should attempt to verify all this by experiment would forget the difference of the human and divine nature. For God only has the knowledge and also the power which are able to combine many things into one and again resolve the one into many. But no man either is or ever will be able to accomplish either the one or the other operation.

These are the elements, thus of necessity then subsisting, which the creator of the fairest and best of created things associated with himself when he made the self-sufficing and most perfect god, using the necessary causes as his ministers in the accomplishment of his work, but himself contriving the good in all his creations. Wherefore we may distinguish two sorts of causes, the one divine and the other necessary, and may seek for the divine in all things, as far as our nature admits, with a view to the blessed life; but the necessary kind only for the sake of the divine, considering that without them and when isolated from them, these higher things for which we look cannot be apprehended or received or in any way shared by us.

Seeing, then, that we have now prepared for our use the various classes of causes which are the material out of which the remainder of our discourse must be woven, just as wood is the material of the carpenter, let us revert in a few words to the point at which we began, and then endeavor to add on a suitable ending to the beginning of our tale.

As I said at first, when all things were in disorder, God created in each thing in relation to itself, and in all things in relation to each other, all the measures and harmonies which they could possibly receive. For in those days nothing had any proportion except by accident; nor did any of the things which now have names deserve to be named at all—as, for example, fire, water, and the rest of the elements. All these the creator first set in order, and out of them he constructed the universe, which was a single animal comprehending in itself all other aninals, mortal and immortal. Now of the divine, he himself was the creator, but the creation of the mortal he committed to his offspring. And they, imitating him, received from him the immortal principle of the soul; and around this they proceeded to fashion a mortal body, and made it to be the vehicle of the soul, and constructed within the body a soul of another na-

69

52

ture which was mortal, subject to terrible and irresistible affections —first of all, pleasure, the greatest incitement to evil; then, pain, which deters from good; also rashness and fear, two foolish counselors, anger hard to be appeased, and hope easily led astray— these they mingled with irrational sense and with all-daring love[30] according to necessary laws, and so framed man. Wherefore, fearing to pollute the divine any more than was absolutely unavoidable, they gave to the mortal nature a separate habitation in another part of the body, placing the neck between them to be the isthmus and boundary, which they constructed between the head and breast, to keep them apart. And in the breast, and in what is termed the thorax, they encased the mortal soul; and as the one part of this was superior and the other inferior they divided the cavity of the thorax into two parts, as the women's and men's apartments are divided in houses, and placed the midriff to be a wall of partition between them. That part of the inferior soul which is endowed with courage and passion and loves contention, they settled nearer the head, midway between the midriff and the neck, in order that it might be under the rule of reason and might join with it in controlling and restraining the desires when they are no longer willing of their own accord to obey the word of command issuing from the citadel.

The heart, the knot[31] of the veins and the fountain of the blood which races through all the limbs, was set in the place of guard, that, when the might of passion was roused by reason making proclamation of any wrong assailing them from without or being perpetrated by the desires within, quickly the whole power of feeling in the body, perceiving these commands and threats, might obey and follow through every turn and alley, and thus allow the principle of the best to have the command in all of them. But the gods, foreknowing that the palpitation of the heart in the expectation of danger and the swelling and excitement of passion was caused by fire, formed and implanted as a supporter to the heart the lung, which was, in the first place, soft and bloodless, and also had within hollows like the pores of a sponge, in order that by receiving the breath and the drink, it might give coolness and the power

[30] Putting a colon after εὐπαράγωγον and reading αἰσθήει δὲ ἀλόγῳ.
[31] Reading ἄμμα.

of respiration and alleviate the heat. Wherefore they cut the air-channels leading to the lung, and placed the lung about the heart as a soft spring, that, when passion was rife within, the heart, beating against a yielding body, might be cooled and suffer less, and might thus become more ready to join with passion in the service of reason.

The part of the soul which desires meats and drinks and the other things of which it has need by reason of the bodily nature, they placed between the midriff and the boundary of the navel, contriving in all this region a sort of manger for the food of the body; and there they bound it down like a wild animal which was chained up with man, and must be nourished if man was to exist. They appointed this lower creation his place here in order that he might be always feeding at the manger, and have his dwelling as far as might be from the council-chamber, making as little noise and disturbance as possible, and permitting the best part to advise quietly for the good of the whole. And knowing that this lower principle in man would not comprehend reason, and even if attaining to some degree of perception would never naturally care for rational notions, but that it would be led away by phantoms and visions night and day—to be a remedy for this, God combined with it the liver and placed it in the house of the lower nature, contriving that it should be solid and smooth, and bright and sweet, and should also have a bitter quality in order that the power of thought, which proceeds from the mind, might be reflected as in a mirror which receives likenesses of objects and gives back images of them to the sight; and so might strike terror into the desires when, making use of the bitter part of the liver, to which it is akin, it comes threatening and invading, and diffusing this bitter element swiftly through the whole liver produces colors like bile, and contracting every part makes it wrinkled and rough; and twisting out of its right place and contorting the lobe and closing and shutting up the vessels and gates causes pain and loathing. And the converse happens when some gentle inspiration of the understanding pictures images of an opposite character, and allays the bile and bitterness by refusing to stir or touch the nature opposed to itself, but by making use of the natural sweetness of the liver corrects all things

71

and makes them to be right and smooth and free, and renders the portion of the soul which resides about the liver happy and joyful, enabling it to pass the night in peace, and to practise divination in sleep, inasmuch as it has no share in mind and reason. For the authors of our being, remembering the command of their father when he bade them create the human race as good as they could, that they might correct our inferior parts and make them to attain a measure of truth, placed in the liver the seat of divination. And herein is a proof that God has given the art of divination not to the wisdom, but to the foolishness of man. No man, when in his wits, attains prophetic truth and inspiration; but when he receives the inspired word, either his intelligence is enthralled in sleep or he is demented by some distemper or possession. And he who would understand what he remembers to have been said, whether in a 72 dream or when he was awake, by the prophetic and inspired nature, or would determine by reason the meaning of the apparitions which he has seen, and what indications they afford to this man or that, of past, present or future good and evil, must first recover his wits. But, while he continues demented, he cannot judge of the visions which he sees or the words which he utters; the ancient saying is very true—that "only a man who has his wits can act or judge about himself and his own affairs." And for this reason it is customary to appoint interpreters to be judges of the true inspiration. Some persons call them prophets; they are quite unaware that they are only the expositors of dark sayings and visions, and are not to be called prophets at all, but only interpreters of prophecy.

Such is the nature of the liver, which is placed as we have described in order that it may give prophetic intimations. During the life of each individual these intimations are plainer, but after his death the liver becomes blind and delivers oracles too obscure to be intelligible. The neighboring organ [the spleen] is situated on the left-hand side and is constructed with a view of keeping the liver bright and pure—like a napkin, always ready prepared and at hand to clean the mirror. And hence, when any impurities arise in the region of the liver by reason of disorders of the body, the loose nature of the spleen, which is composed of a hollow and blood-less tissue, receives them all and clears them away, and when filled with the unclean matter, swells and festers, but, again, when the body is purged, settles down into the same place as before, and is humbled.

Concerning the soul, as to which part is mortal and which divine, and how and why they are separated, and where located, if God acknowledges that we have spoken the truth, then, and then only, can we be confident; still, we may venture to assert that what has been said by us is probable, and will be rendered more probable by investigation. Let us assume this much.

The creation of the rest of the body follows next in order, and this we may investigate in a similar manner. And it appears to be very meet that the body should be framed on the following principles:

The authors of our race were aware that we should be intemperate in eating and drinking and take a good deal more than was necessary or proper, by reason of gluttony. In order then that disease might not quickly destroy us, and lest our mortal race should perish without fulfilling its end—intending to provide against this, the gods made what is called the lower belly, to be a receptacle for the superfluous meat and drink, and formed the convolution of the bowels, so that the food might be prevented from passing quickly through and compelling the body to require more food, thus producing insatiable gluttony and making the whole race an enemy to philosophy and music, and rebellious against the divinest element within us.

The bones and flesh, and other similar parts of us, were made as follows. The first principle of all of them was the generation of the marrow. For the bonds of life which unite the soul with the body are made fast there, and they are the root and foundation of the human race. The marrow itself is created out of other materials: God took such of the primary triangles as were straight and smooth and were adapted by their perfection to produce fire and water, and air and earth—these, I say, he separated from their kinds, and mingling them in due proportions with one another, made the marrow out of them to be a universal seed of the whole race of mankind; and in this seed he then planted and enclosed the souls, and in the original distribution gave to the marrow as many and various forms as the different kinds of souls were hereafter to receive. That which, like a field, was to receive the divine seed, he made round every way, and called that portion of the marrow "brain," intending that, when an animal was perfected, the vessel containing this substance should be the head; but that which was intended to contain the remaining and mortal part of the soul he distributed into figures at once round and elongated, and he called them all by the name "marrow"; and to these, as to anchors, fastening the bonds of the whole soul, he proceeded to fashion around them the entire framework of our body, constructing for the marrow, first of all, a complete covering of bone.

Bone was composed by him in the following manner: having sifted pure and smooth earth he kneaded it and wetted it with marrow, and after that he put it into fire and then into water, and once more into fire and again into water—in this way, by frequent transfers from one to the other, he made it insoluble by either. Out of this he fashioned, as in a lathe, a globe made of bone, which he placed around the brain, and in this he left a narrow opening; and around the marrow of the neck and back he formed vertebrae which he placed under one another like pivots, beginning at the head and extending through the whole of the trunk. Thus wishing to preserve the entire seed, he enclosed it in a stone-like casing, inserting joints, and using in the formation of them the power of the other or diverse as an intermediate nature, that they might have motion and flexure. Then again, considering that the bone would be too brittle and inflexible, and when heated and again cooled would soon mortify and destroy the seed within—having this in view, he contrived the sinews and the flesh, that so binding all the members together by the sinews, which admitted of being stretched and relaxed about the vertebrae, he might thus make the body capable of flexion and extension, while the flesh would serve as a protection against the summer heat and against the winter cold, and also against falls, softly and easily yielding to external bodies, like articles made of felt; and containing in itself a warm moisture which in summer exudes and makes the surface damp, would impart a natural coolness to the whole body; and again in winter by the help of this internal warmth would form a very tolerable defense against the frost which surrounds it and attacks it from without. He who modeled us, considering these things, mixed earth with fire and water and blended them; and making a ferment of acid and salt, he mingled it with them and formed soft and succulent flesh. As for the sinews, he made them of a mixture of bone and unfermented flesh, attempered so as to be in a mean, and gave them a yellow color; wherefore the sinews have a firmer and more glutinous nature than flesh, but a softer and moister nature than the bones. With these God covered the bones and marrow, binding them together by sinews, and then enshrouded them all in an upper covering of flesh. The more living and sensitive of the bones he enclosed in the thinnest film of flesh, and those which had the least life within them in the thickest and most solid flesh. So again on the joints of the bones, where reason indicated that no more was required, he placed only a thin covering of flesh, that it might not interfere with the flexion of our bodies and make them unwieldy because difficult to move; and also that it might not, by being crowded and pressed and matted together, destroy sensation by reason of its hardness, and impair the memory and dull the edge of intelligence. Wherefore also the thighs and the shanks and the hips, and the bones of the arms and the forearms, and other parts which have no joints, and the inner bones, which on account of the rarity of the soul in the marrow are destitute of reason—all these are abundantly provided with flesh; but such as have mind in them are in general less fleshy, except where the creator has made some part solely of flesh in order to give sensation—as, for example, the tongue. But commonly this is not the case. For the nature which comes into being and grows up in us by a law of necessity does not admit of the combination of solid bone and much flesh with acute perceptions. More than any other part, the framework of the head would have had them if they could have co-existed, and the human race, having a strong and fleshy and sinewy head, would have had a life twice or many times as long as it now has, and also more healthy and free from pain. But our creators, considering whether they should make a longer-lived race which was worse, or a shorter-lived race which was better, came to the conclusion that every one ought to prefer a shorter span of life, which was better, to a longer one, which was worse; and therefore they covered the head with thin bone, but not with flesh and sinews, since it had no joints; and thus the head was added, having more wisdom and sensation than the rest of the body, but also being in every man far weaker. For these reasons and after this manner God placed the sinews at the extremity of the head, in a circle round the neck, and glued them together by the principle of likeness and fastened the extremities of the jawbones to them below the face, and the other sinews he dispersed throughout the body, fastening limb to limb. The framers of us framed the mouth, as now arranged, having teeth and tongue and lips, with a view to the necessary and the good, contriving the way in for necessary purposes, the way out for the best purposes; for that is necessary which enters in and gives food to the body; but the river of speech, which flows out of a man and ministers to the intelligence, is the fairest and noblest of all streams. Still the head could neither be left a bare frame of bones, on account of the extremes of heat and cold in the different seasons, nor yet be allowed to be wholly covered and so become dull and senseless by reason of an overgrowth of flesh. The fleshy nature was not therefore wholly dried up, but a large sort of peel was parted off and 76 remained over, which is now called the skin. This met and grew by the help of the cerebral moisture, and became the circular envelopment of the head. And the moisture, rising up under the sutures, watered and closed in the skin upon the crown, forming a sort of knot. The diversity of the sutures was caused by the power of the courses of the soul and of the food, and the more these struggled against one another, the more numerous they became, and fewer if the struggle were less violent. This skin the divine power pierced all round with fire, and out of the punctures which were thus made the moisture issued forth, and the liquid and heat which was pure came away, and a mixed part which was composed of the same material as the skin, and had a fineness equal to the punctures, was borne up by its own impulse and extended far outside the head, but, being too slow to escape, was thrust back by the external air and rolled up underneath the skin, where it took root. Thus the hair sprang up in the skin, being akin to it because it is like threads of leather, but rendered harder and closer through the pressure of the cold, by which each hair, while in process of separation from the skin, is compressed and cooled. Wherefore the creator formed the head hairy, making use of the causes which I have mentioned, and reflecting also that instead of flesh the brain needed the hair to be a light covering or guard which would give shade in summer and shelter in winter, and at the same time would not impede our quickness of perception. From the combination of sinew, skin, and bone, in the structure of the finger, there arises a triple compound which, when dried up, takes the form of one hard skin partaking of all three natures, and was fabricated by these second causes, but designed by mind which is the principal cause with an eye to the future. For our creators well knew that women and other animals would some day be framed out of men, and they further knew that many animals would require the use of nails for many purposes; wherefore they fashioned in men at their first creation the rudiments of nails. For this purpose and for these reasons they caused skin, hair, and nails to grow at the extremities of the limbs.

77 And now that all the parts and members of the mortal animal had come together, since its life of necessity consisted of fire and breath, and it therefore wasted away by dissolution and depletion, the gods contrived the following remedy: They mingled a nature akin to that of man with other forms and perceptions and thus created another kind of animal. These are the trees and plants and seeds which have been improved by cultivation and are now domesticated among us; anciently there were only the wild kinds, which are older than the cultivated. For everything that partakes of life may be truly called a living being, and the animal of which we are now speaking partakes of the third kind of soul, which is said to be seated between the midriff and the navel, having no part in opinion or reason or mind, but only in feelings of pleasure and pain and the desires which accompany them. For this nature is always in a passive state, revolving in and about itself, repelling the motion from without and using its own, and accordingly is not endowed by nature with the power of observing or reflecting on its own concerns. Wherefore it lives and does not differ from a living being, but is fixed and rooted in the same spot, having no power of self-motion.

Now after the superior powers had created all these natures to be food for us who are of the inferior nature, they cut various channels through the body as through a garden, that it might be watered as from a running stream. In the first place, they cut two hidden channels or veins down the back where the skin and the flesh join, which answered severally to the right and left side of the body.

These they let down along the backbone, so as to have the marrow of generation between them, where it was most likely to flourish, and in order that the stream coming down from above might flow freely to the other parts, and equalize the irrigation. In the next place, they divided the veins about the head, and interlacing them, they sent them in opposite directions; those coming from the right side they sent to the left of the body, and those from the left they diverted toward the right, so that they and the skin might together form a bond which should fasten the head to the body, since the crown of the head was not encircled by sinews; and also in order that the sensations from both sides might be distributed over the whole body. And next, they ordered the watercourses of the body in a manner which I will describe, and which will be more easily understood if we begin by admitting that all things which have lesser parts retain the greater, but the greater cannot retain the lesser. Now of all natures fire has the smallest parts, and therefore penetrates through earth and water and air and their compounds, nor can anything hold it. And a similar principle applies to the human belly; for when meats and drinks enter it, it holds them, but it cannot hold air and fire because the particles of which they consist are smaller than its own structure.

These elements, therefore, God employed for the sake of distributing moisture from the belly into the veins, weaving together a network of fire and air like a weel, having at the entrance two lesser weels; further he constructed one of these with two openings, and from the lesser weels he extended cords reaching all round to the extremities of the network. All the interior of the net he made of fire, but the lesser weels and their cavity, of air. The network he took and spread over the newly-formed animal in the following manner: he let the lesser weels pass into the mouth; there were two of them, and one he let down by the air-pipes into the lungs, the other by the side of the air-pipes into the belly. The former he divided into two branches, both of which he made to meet at the channels of the nose, so that when the way through the mouth did not act, the streams of the mouth as well were replenished through the nose. With the other cavity [that is, of the greater weel] he enveloped the hollow parts of the body, and at one time he made all this to flow into the lesser weels, quite gently, for they are composed of

78

air, and at another time he caused the lesser weels to flow back again; and the net he made to find a way in and out through the pores of the body, and the rays of fire which are bound fast within followed the passage of the air either way, never at any time ceasing so long as the mortal being holds together. This process, as we affirm, the name-giver named inspiration and expiration. And all this movement, active as well as passive, takes place in order that the body, being watered and cooled, may receive nourishment and life; for when the respiration is going in and out, and the fire, which is fast bound within, follows it, and ever and anon moving to and fro, enters through the belly and reaches the meat and drink, it dissolves them, and dividing them into small portions and guiding them through the passages where it goes, pumps them as from a fountain into the channels of the veins, and makes the stream of the veins flow through the body as through a conduit.

Let us once more consider the phenomena of respiration, and inquire into the causes which have made it what it is. They are as follows: seeing that there is no such thing as a vacuum into which any of those things which are moved can enter, and the breath is carried from us into the external air, the next point is, as will be clear to every one, that it does not go into a vacant space, but pushes its neighbor out of its place, and that which is thrust out in turn drives out its neighbor; and in this way everything of necessity at last comes round to that place from whence the breath came forth, and enters in there and following the breath fills up the vacant space; and this goes on like the rotation of a wheel, because there can be no such thing as a vacuum. Wherefore also the breast and the lungs, when they emit the breath, are replenished by the air which surrounds the body and which enters in through the pores of the flesh and is driven round in a circle; and again, the air which is sent away and passes out through the body forces the breath inwards through the passage of the mouth and the nostrils. Now the origin of this movement may be supposed to be as follows: in the interior of every animal the hottest part is that which is around the blood and veins; it is in a manner an internal fountain of fire, which we compare to the network of a creel, being woven all of fire and extended through the center of the body, while the outer parts are composed of air. Now we must admit that

79

heat naturally proceeds outward to its own place and to its kindred element; and as there are two exits for the heat, the one out through the body, and the other through the mouth and nostrils, when it moves toward the one, it drives round the air at the other, and that which is driven round falls into the fire and becomes warm, and that which goes forth is cooled. But when the heat changes its place, and the particles at the other exit grow warmer, the hotter air inclining in that direction and carried toward its native element, fire, pushes round the air at the other; and this being affected in the same way and communicating the same impulse, a circular motion swaying to and fro is produced by the double process, which we call inspiration and expiration.

The phenomena of medical cupping-glasses and of the swallowing of drink and of the projection of bodies, whether discharged in the air or bowled along the ground, are to be investigated on a similar principle; and swift and slow sounds, which appear to be high and low, and are sometimes discordant on account of their inequality, and then again harmonical on account of the equality of the motion which they excite in us. For when the motions of the antecedent swifter sounds begin to pause and the two are equalized, the slower sounds overtake the swifter and then propel them. When they overtake them they do not intrude a new and discordant motion, but introduce the beginnings of a slower which answers to the swifter as it dies away, thus producing a single mixed expression out of high and low, whence arises a pleasure which even the unwise feel, and which to the wise becomes a higher sort of delight, being an imitation of divine harmony in mortal motions. Moreover, as to the flowing of water, the fall of the thunderbolt, and the marvels that are observed about the attraction of amber and the Heraclean stones—in none of these cases is there any attraction; but he who investigates rightly will find that such wonderful phenomena are attributable to the combination of certain conditions—the non-existence of a vacuum, the fact that objects push one another round, and that they change places, passing severally into their proper positions as they are divided or combined.

Such, as we have seen, is the nature and such are the causes of respiration—the subject in which this discussion originated. For the fire cuts the food and following the breath surges up within, fire and breath rising together and filling the veins by drawing up out of the belly and pouring into them the cut portions of the food; and so the streams of food are kept flowing through the whole body in all animals. And fresh cuttings from kindred substances, whether the fruits of the earth or herb of the field, which God planted to be our daily food, acquire all sorts of colors by their intermixture; but red is the most pervading of them, being created by the cutting action of fire and by the impression which it makes on a moist substance; and hence the liquid which circulates in the body has a color such as we have described. The liquid itself we call blood, which nourishes the flesh and the whole body, whence all parts are watered and empty places filled.

81

Now the process of repletion and evacuation is effected after the manner of the universal motion by which all kindred substances are drawn towards one another. For the external elements which surround us are always causing us to consume away and distributing and sending off like to like; the particles of blood, too, which are divided and contained within the frame of the animal as in a sort of heaven, are compelled to imitate the motion of the universe. Each, therefore, of the divided parts within us, being carried to its kindred nature, replenishes the void. When more is taken away than flows in, then we decay, and when less, we grow and increase.

The frame of the entire creature when young has the triangles of each kind new, and may be compared to the keel of a vessel which is just off the stocks; they are locked firmly together and yet the whole mass is soft and delicate, being freshly formed of marrow and nurtured on milk. Now when the triangles out of which meats and drinks are composed come in from without, and are comprehended in the body, being older and weaker than the triangles already there, the frame of the body gets the better of them and its newer triangles cut them up, and so the animal grows great, being nourished by a multitude of similar particles. But when the roots of the triangles are loosened by having undergone many conflicts with many things in the course of time, they are no longer able to cut or assimilate the food which enters, but are themselves easily divided by the bodies which come in from without. In this way every animal is overcome and decays, and this affection is called old age. And at last, when the bonds by which the triangles of the marrow are united no longer hold and are parted by the strain of existence, they in turn loosen the bonds of the soul, and she, obtaining a natural release, flies away with joy. For that which takes place according to nature is pleasant, but that which is contrary to nature is painful. And thus death, if caused by disease or produced by wounds, is painful and violent; but that sort of death which comes with old age and fulfills the debt of nature is the easiest of deaths, and is accompanied with pleasure rather than with pain.

Now everyone can see whence diseases arise. There are four natures out of which the body is compacted—earth and fire and water and air—and the unnatural excess or defect of these, or the change of any of them from its own natural place into another, or, since there are more kinds than one of fire and of the other elements, the assumption by any of these of a wrong kind, or any similar irregularity, produces disorders and diseases; for when any of them is produced or changed in a manner contrary to nature, the parts which were previously cool grow warm, and those which were dry become moist, and the light become heavy, and the heavy light; all sorts of changes occur. For, as we affirm, a thing can only remain the same with itself, whole and sound, when the same is added to it, or subtracted from it, in the same respect and in the same manner and in due proportion; and whatever comes or goes away in violation of these laws causes all manner of changes and infinite diseases and corruptions. Now there is a second class of structures which are also natural, and this affords a second opportunity of observing diseases to him who would understand them. For whereas marrow and bone and flesh and sinews are composed of the four elements, and the blood, though after another manner, is likewise formed out of them, most diseases originate in the way which I have described; but the worst of all owe their severity to the fact that the generation of these substances proceeds in a wrong order; they are then destroyed. For the natural order is that the flesh and sinews should be made of blood, the sinews out of the fibers to which they are akin, and the flesh out of the clots which are formed when the fibers are separated. And the glutinous and rich matter which comes away from the sinews and the flesh, not only glues the flesh to the bones, but nourishes and imparts growth to the bone which surrounds the marrow; and by reason of the solidity of the bones, that which filters through consists of the purest and smoothest and oiliest sort of triangles, dropping like dew from the bones and watering the marrow. Now when each process takes place in this order, health commonly results; when in the opposite order, disease. For when the flesh becomes decomposed and sends back the wasting substance into the veins, then an oversupply of blood of diverse kinds, mingling with air in the veins, having variegated colors and bitter properties as well as acid and saline qualities, contains all sorts of bile and serum and phlegm. For all things go the wrong way, and having become corrupted, first, they taint the blood itself, and then ceasing to give nourishment to the body they are carried along the veins in all directions, no longer preserving the order of their natural courses, but at war with themselves, because they receive no good from one another, and are hostile to the abiding constitution of the body, which they corrupt and dissolve. The oldest part of the flesh which is corrupted, being hard to decompose, from long burning grows black, and from being everywhere corroded becomes bitter, and is injurious to every part of the body which is still uncorrupted. Sometimes, when the bitter element is refined away, the black part assumes an acidity which takes the place of the bitterness; at other times the bitterness being tinged with blood has a redder color; and this, when mixed with black, takes the hue of grass[32]; and again, an auburn color mingles with the bitter matter when new flesh is decomposed by the fire which surrounds the internal flame—to all which symptoms some physician, perhaps, or rather some philosopher who had the power of seeing in many dissimilar things one nature deserving of a name has assigned the common name of bile. But the other kinds of bile are variously distinguished by their colors. As for serum, that sort which is the watery part of blood is innocent, but that which is a secretion of black and acid bile is malignant when mingled by the power of heat with any salt substance, and is then called acid phlegm. Again, the substance which is formed by the liquefaction of new and tender flesh when air is present, if inflated and encased in liquid so as to form bubbles which separately are invisible owing to their small size, but when collected are of a bulk which is visible and have a white color arising out of the generation

[32] Reading χλοῶδες.

83

of foam—all this decomposition of tender flesh when intermingled with air is termed by us white phlegm. And the whey or sediment of newly-formed phlegm is sweat and tears, and includes the various daily discharges by which the body is purified. Now all these become causes of disease when the blood is not replenished in a natural manner by food and drink, but gains bulk from opposite sources in violation of the laws of nature. When the several parts of the flesh are separated by disease, if the foundation remains, the power of the disorder is only half as great, and there is still a prospect of an easy recovery; but when that which binds the flesh to the bones is diseased, and no longer being separated from the muscles and sinews,[33] ceases to give nourishment to the bone and to unite flesh and bone, and from being oily and smooth and glutinous becomes rough and salt and dry, owing to bad regimen, then all the substance thus corrupted crumbles away under the flesh and the sinews and separates from the bone, and the fleshy parts fall away from their foundation and leave the sinews bare and full of brine, and the flesh again gets into the circulation of the blood and makes the previously mentioned disorders still greater. And if these bodily affections be severe, still worse are the prior disorders; as when the bone itself, by reason of the density of the flesh, does not obtain sufficient air, but becomes mouldy and hot and gangrened and receives no nutriment, and the natural process is inverted, and the bone crumbling passes into the food, and the food into the flesh, and the flesh again falling into the blood makes all maladies that may occur more virulent than those already mentioned. But the worst case of all is when the marrow is diseased, either from excess or defect; and this is the cause of the very greatest and most fatal disorders in which the whole course of the body is reversed.

There is a third class of diseases which may be conceived of as arising in three ways; for they are produced sometimes by wind, and sometimes by phlegm, and sometimes by bile. When the lung, which is the dispenser of the air to the body, is obstructed by rheums and its passages are not free, some of them not acting, while through others too much air enters, then the parts which are unrefreshed by air corrode, while in other parts the excess of air

[33] Reading αὐτό for αὖ τό and ἅμα for αἷμα.

forcing its way through the veins distorts them and decomposing the body is enclosed in the midst of it and occupies the midriff; thus numberless painful diseases are produced, accompanied by copious sweats. And oftentimes when the flesh is dissolved in the body, wind, generated within and unable to escape, is the source of quite as much pain as the air coming in from without; but the greatest pain is felt when the wind gets about the sinews and the veins of the shoulders and swells them up, and so twists back the great tendons and the sinews which are connected with them. These disorders are called tetanus and opisthotonus, by reason of the tension which accompanies them. The cure of them is difficult; relief is in most cases given by fever supervening. The white phlegm, though dangerous when detained within by reason of the air-bubbles, yet if it can communicate with the outside air, is less severe, and only discolors the body, generating leprous eruptions and similar diseases. When it is mingled with black bile and dispersed about the courses of the head, which are the divinest part of us, the attack, if coming on in sleep, is not so severe; but when assailing those who are awake it is hard to be got rid of, and being an affection of a sacred part, is most justly called sacred. An acid and salt phlegm, again, is the source of all those diseases which take the form of catarrh, but they have many names because the places into which they flow are manifold.

Inflammations of the body come from burnings and inflamings, and all of them originate in bile. When bile finds a means of discharge, it boils up and sends forth all sorts of tumors; but when imprisoned within, it generates many inflammatory diseases, above all when mingled with pure blood; since it then displaces the fibers which are scattered about in the blood and are designed to maintain the balance of rare and dense, in order that the blood may not be so liquefied by heat as to exude from the pores of the body, nor again become too dense and thus find a difficulty in circulating through the veins. The fibers are so constituted as to maintain this balance; and if any one brings them all together when the blood is dead and in process of cooling, then the blood which remains becomes fluid, but if they are left alone, they soon congeal by reason of the surrounding cold. The fibers having this power over the blood, bile, which is only stale blood, and which from being flesh is dissolved again into blood, at the first influx coming in little by little, hot and liquid, is congealed by the power of the fibers; and so congealing and made to cool, it produces internal cold and shuddering. When it enters with more of a flood and overcomes the fibers by its heat, and boiling up throws them into disorder, if it have power enough to maintain its supremacy, it penetrates the marrow and burns up what may be termed the cables of the soul, and sets her free; but when there is not so much of it, and the body though wasted still holds out, the bile is itself mastered and is either utterly banished or is thrust through the veins into the lower or upper belly, and is driven out of the body like an exile from a state in which there has been civil war; whence arise diarrhoeas and dysenteries, and all such disorders. When the constitution is disordered by excess of fire, continuous heat and fever are the result; when excess of air is the cause, then the fever is quotidian; when of water, which is a more sluggish element than either fire or air, then the fever is a tertian; when of earth, which is the most sluggish of the four, and is only purged away in a fourfold period, the result is a quartan fever, which can with difficulty be shaken off.

Such is the manner in which diseases of the body arise; the disorders of the soul, which depend upon the body, originate as follows: we must acknowledge disease of the mind to be a want of intelligence; and of this there are two kinds; to wit, madness and ignorance. In whatever state a man experiences either of them, that state may be called disease; and excessive pains and pleasures are justly to be regarded as the greatest diseases to which the soul is liable. For a man who is in great joy or in great pain, in his unseasonable eagerness to attain the one and to avoid the other, is not able to see or to hear anything rightly; but he is mad and is at the time utterly incapable of any participation in reason. He who has the seed about the spinal marrow too plentiful and overflowing, like a tree overladen with fruit, has many throes, and also obtains many pleasures in his desires and their offspring, and is for the most part of his life deranged because his pleasures and pains are so very great; his soul is rendered foolish and disordered by his body; yet he is regarded not as one diseased, but as one who is voluntarily bad, which is a mistake. The truth is that the intemperance of love is a disease of the soul due chiefly to the mois-

86

ture and fluidity which is produced in one of the elements by the loose consistency of the bones. And in general, all that which is termed the incontinence of pleasure and is deemed a reproach under the idea that the wicked voluntarily do wrong is not justly a matter for reproach. For no man is voluntarily bad; but the bad become bad by reason of an ill disposition of the body and bad education—things which are hateful to every man and happen to him against his will. And in the case of pain, too, in like manner the soul suffers much evil from the body. For where the acid and briny phlegm and other bitter and bilious humors wander about in the body and find no exit or escape, but are pent up within and mingle their own vapors with the motions of the soul, and are blended with them, they produce all sorts of diseases, more or fewer, and in every degree of intensity; and being carried to the three places of the soul, whichever they may severally assail, they create infinite varieties of ill-temper and melancholy, of rashness and cowardice, and also of forgetfulness and stupidity. Further, when to this evil constitution of body evil forms of government are added and evil discourses are uttered in private as well as in public, and no sort of instruction is given in youth to cure these evils, then all of us who are bad become bad from two causes which are entirely beyond our control. In such cases the planters are to blame rather than the plants, the educators rather than the educated. But however that may be, we should endeavor as far as we can, by education and studies and learning, to avoid vice and attain virtue; this, however, is part of another subject.

There is a corresponding inquiry concerning the mode of treatment by which the mind and the body are to be preserved, about which it is meet and right that I should say a word in turn; for it is more our duty to speak of the good than of the evil. Everything that is good is fair, and the fair is not without proportion, and the animal which is to be fair must have due proportion. Now we perceive lesser symmetries or proportions and reason about them, but of the highest and greatest we take no heed; for there is no proportion or disproportion more productive of health and disease, and virtue and vice, than that between soul and body. This however we do not perceive, nor do we reflect that when a weak or small frame is the vehicle of a great and mighty soul, or conversely, when a little soul is encased in a large body, then the whole animal is not fair, for it lacks the most important of all symmetries; but the due proportion of mind and body is the fairest and loveliest of all sights to him who has the seeing eye. Just as a body which has a leg too long, or which is unsymmetrical in some other respect, is an unpleasant sight, and also, when doing its share of work, is much distressed and makes convulsive efforts, and often stumbles through awkwardness, and is the cause of infinite evil to its own self—in like manner we should conceive of the double nature which we call the living being; and when in this compound there is an impassioned soul more powerful than the body, that soul, I say, 88 convulses and fills with disorders the whole inner nature of man, and when eager in the pursuit of some sort of learning or study, causes wasting; or again, when teaching or disputing in private or in public, and strifes and controversies arise, inflames and dissolves the composite frame of man and introduces rheums; and the nature of this phenomenon is not understood by most professors of medicine, who ascribe it to the opposite of the real cause. And once more, when a body large and too strong for the soul is united to a small and weak intelligence, then inasmuch as there are two desires natural to man—one of food for the sake of the body, and one of wisdom for the sake of the diviner part of us—then, I say, the motions of the stronger, getting the better and increasing their own power, but making the soul dull and stupid and forgetful, engender ignorance, which is the greatest of diseases. There is one protection against both kinds of disproportion—that we should not move the body without the soul or the soul without the body, and thus they will be on their guard against each other and be healthy and well balanced. And therefore the mathematician or any one else whose thoughts are much absorbed in some intellectual pursuit, must allow his body also to have due exercise, and practise gymnastic; and he who is careful to fashion the body should in turn impart to the soul its proper motions and should cultivate music and all philosophy if he would deserve to be called truly fair and truly good. And the separate parts should be treated in the same manner, in imitation of the pattern of the universe; for as the body is heated and also cooled within by the elements which enter into it, and is again dried up and moistened by external things, and experiences these and the like affections from both kinds of motions, the result is that the body if given up to motion when in a state of quiescence is overmastered and perishes; but if any one, in imitation of that which we call the foster-mother and nurse of the universe, will not allow the body ever to be inactive, but is always producing motions and agitations through its whole extent, which form the natural defense against other motions both internal and external, and by moderate exercise reduces to order according to their affinities the particles and affections which are wandering about the body, as we have already said when speaking of the universe,[34] he will not allow enemy placed by the side of enemy to stir up wars and disorders in the body, but he will place friend by the side of friend, so as to create health. Now of all motions that is the best which is produced in a thing by itself, for it is most akin to the motion of thought and of the universe; but that motion which is caused by others is not so good, and worst of all is that which moves the body, when at rest, in parts only and by some external agency. Wherefore of all modes of purifying and re-uniting the body the best is gymnastic; the next best is a surging motion, as in sailing or any other mode of conveyance which is not fatiguing; the third sort of motion may be of use in a case of extreme necessity, but in any other will be adopted by no man of sense: I mean the purgative treatment of physicians; for diseases unless they are very dangerous should not be irritated by medicines, since every form of disease is in a manner akin to the living being, whose complex frame has an appointed term of life. For not the whole race only, but each individual—barring inevitable accidents—comes into the world having a fixed span, and the triangles in us are originally framed with power to last for a certain time beyond which no man can prolong his life. And this holds also of the constitution of diseases; if any one regardless of the appointed time tries to subdue them by medicine, he only aggravates and multiplies them. Wherefore we ought always to manage them by regimen, as far as a man can spare the time, and not provoke a disagreeable enemy by medicines.

Enough of the composite animal and of the body which is a part of him, and of the manner in which a man may train and be

[34] *Supra,* 33a.

trained by himself so as to live most according to reason; and we must above and before all provide that the element which is to train him shall be the fairest and best adapted to that purpose. A minute discussion of this subject would be a serious task; but if, as before, I am to give only an outline, the subject may not unfitly be summed up as follows:

I have often remarked that there are three kinds of soul located within us, having each of them motions, and I must now repeat, in the fewest words possible, that one part, if remaining inactive and ceasing from its natural motion, must necessarily become very weak, but that which is trained and exercised, very strong. Wherefore we should take care that the movements of the different parts 90 of the soul should be in due proportion.

And we should consider that God gave the sovereign part of the human soul to be the divinity of each one, being that part which, as we say, dwells at the top of the body, and inasmuch as we are a plant not of an earthly but of a heavenly growth, raises us from earth to our kindred who are in heaven. And in this we say truly; for the divine power suspended the head and root of us from that place where the generation of the soul first began, and thus made the whole body upright. When a man is always occupied with the cravings of desire and ambition, and is eagerly striving to satisfy them, all his thoughts must be mortal, and, as far as it is possible altogether to become such, he must be mortal every whit because he has cherished his mortal part. But he who has been earnest in the love of knowledge and of true wisdom, and has exercised his intellect more than any other part of him, must have thoughts immortal and divine, if he attain truth, and in so far as human nature is capable of sharing in immortality, he must altogether be immortal; and since he is ever cherishing the divine power and has the divinity within him in perfect order, he will be perfectly happy. Now there is only one way of taking care of things, and this is to give to each the food and motion which are natural to it. And the motions which are naturally akin to the divine principle within us are the thoughts and revolutions of the universe. These each man should follow, and correct the courses of the head which were corrupted at our birth, and by learning the harmonies and revolutions of the universe, should assimilate the thinking being to the thought, renewing his original nature, and having assimilated them should attain to that perfect life which the gods have set before mankind, both for the present and the future.

Thus our original design of discoursing about the universe down to the creation of man is nearly completed. A brief mention may be made of the generation of other animals, so far as the subject admits of brevity; in this manner our argument will best attain a due proportion. On the subject of animals, then, the following remarks may be offered: Of the men who came into the world, those who were cowards or led unrighteous lives may with reason be supposed to have changed into the nature of women in the second generation. And this was the reason why at that time the gods created in us the desire of sexual intercourse, contriving in man one animated substance, and in woman another, which they formed respectively in the following manner: The outlet for drink by which liquids pass through the lung under the kidneys and into the bladder, which receives and then by the pressure of the air emits them, was so fashioned by them as to penetrate also into the body of the marrow, which passes from the head along the neck and through the back, and which in the preceding discourse we have named the seed. And the seed, having life and becoming endowed with respiration, produces in that part in which it respires a lively desire of emission, and thus creates in us the love of procreation. Wherefore also in men the organ of generation becoming rebellious and masterful, like an animal disobedient to reason, and maddened with the sting of lust, seeks to gain absolute sway; and the same is the case with the so-called womb or matrix of women; the animal within them is desirous of procreating children, and when remaining unfruitful long beyond its proper time, gets discontented and angry, and wandering in every direction through the body, closes up the passages of the breath, and, by obstructing respiration, drives them to extremity, causing all varieties of disease, until at length the desire and love of the man and the woman, bringing them together[35] and as it were plucking the fruit from the tree, sow in the womb, as in a field, animals unseen by reason of their smallness and without form; these again are separated and matured within; they are then finally brought out into the light, and thus the generation of animals is completed.

[35] Reading ξυνδυάζοντες [conj. Hermann].

Thus were created women and the female sex in general. But the race of birds was created out of innocent light-minded men who, although their minds were directed toward heaven, imagined, in their simplicity, that the clearest demonstration of the things above was to be obtained by sight; these were remodeled and transformed into birds, and they grew feathers instead of hair. The race of wild pedestrian animals, again, came from those who had no philosophy in any of their thoughts, and never considered at all about the nature of the heavens, because they had ceased to use the courses of the head, but followed the guidance of those parts of the soul which are in the breast. In consequence of these habits of theirs they had their front legs and their heads resting upon the earth to which they were drawn by natural affinity; and the crowns of their heads were elongated and of all sorts of shapes, into which the courses of the soul were crushed by reason of disuse. And this was the reason why they were created quadrupeds and polypods: 92 God gave the more senseless of them the more support that they might be more attracted to the earth. And the most foolish of them, who trail their bodies entirely upon the ground and have no longer any need of feet, he made without feet to crawl upon the earth. The fourth class were the inhabitants of the water: these were made out of the most entirely senseless and ignorant of all, whom the transformers did not think any longer worthy of pure respiration, because they possessed a soul which was made impure by all sorts of transgression; and instead of the subtle and pure medium of air, they gave them the deep and muddy sea to be their element of respiration; and hence arose the race of fishes and oysters, and other aquatic animals, which have received the most remote habitations as a punishment of their outlandish ignorance. These are the laws by which animals pass into one another, now, as ever, changing as they lose or gain wisdom and folly.

We may now say that our discourse about the nature of the universe has an end. The world has received animals, mortal and immortal, and is fulfilled with them, and has become a visible animal containing the visible—the sensible God who is the image of the intellectual,[36] the greatest, best, fairest, most perfect—the one only-begotten heaven.

[36] Or reading ποιητοῦ—"of his maker."